Department

M ... 983

Me ... and X

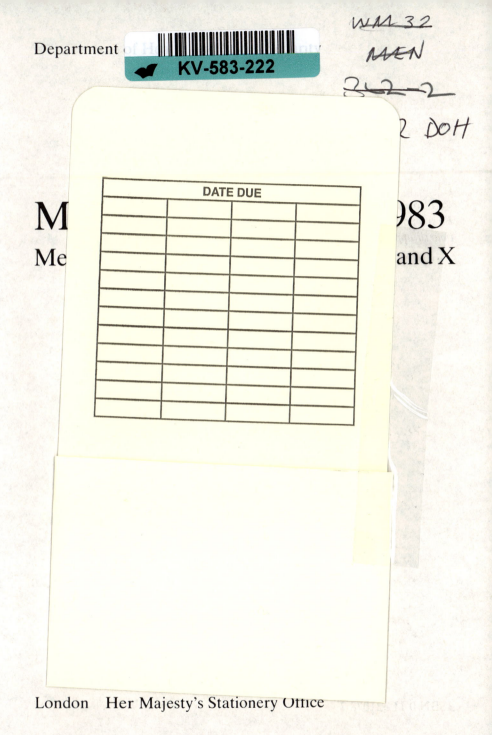

DATE DUE

London   Her Majesty's Stationery Office

ISBN 0 11 321078 7

Mental Health Act 1983

Explanatory memorandum to health authorities, local social service authorities and General Practitioners on Parts I, II, III, IV, V, VI, VIII and X of the Act and associated Schedules, and on the Mental Health (Hospital, Guardianship and Consent to Treatment) Regulations 1983.

Contents

Paragraphs

Mental Health Act 1983
Explanatory Memorandum

Introduction

1   This memorandum describes the main provisions of the Mental Health Act 1983. In particular, it draws attention to the main changes made to the Mental Health Act 1959, by the Mental Health (Amendment) Act 1982. All these changes were consolidated in the Mental Health Act 1983 which took effect from 30 September 1983 when the 1959 and 1982 Acts were largely[1] repealed.

2   The memorandum is for the guidance of all those who work with the Act. It cannot provide an authoritative interpretation of the law or override the statutory provisions of the Act and Regulations. Nor does it describe every detail of the Act, Regulations and Rules which must be referred to when necessary. It does not cover Part VII of the Act which deals with the management of the property and affairs of patients and the Court of Protection, or Part IX which deals with offences.

The Act

3   The Act came into operation with very few exceptions on 30 September 1983. The main exceptions were that mental welfare officers were replaced by approved social workers on 28 October 1984 (see paras 248–249 below) and the new remands to hospital for report or treatment and interim hospital orders were introduced from 1 October 1984.

The Mental Health (Hospital, Guardianship and Consent to Treatment) Regulations 1983

4   These regulations also came into force on 30 September 1983 when The Mental Health (Hospital and Guardianship) Regulations 1960 were

---

[1] Sections 8, 9 and 128 of the 1959 Act, dealing with local authority services, and sexual intercourse with patients, remain in force. However, it is intended eventually to consolidate them into other legislation.

revoked. The regulations, and forms which are prescribed in the regulations, are referred to where appropriate in this memorandum.

References

5   The 1983 Act is divided into ten parts and six schedules. It can be seen from the table of contents that this memorandum generally follows the order in which provisions appear in the Act. Except where specified, references to parts, sections and schedules in this Memorandum are references to parts, sections and schedules of the Mental Health Act 1983, and references to regulations are references to the Hospital, Guardianship and Consent to Treatment Regulations 1983. References to the '1959 Act' or the previous legislation are references to the Mental Health Act 1959. Little reference is made to the Mental Health (Amendment) Act 1982 as the changes made by that Act have been consolidated in the 1983 Act.

Interpretations

6   Many of the definitions used in the Act are to be found in Section 145(1). However, these may be varied in certain parts of the Act, and where this happens the definitions that apply may usually be found in the interpretation Section of that Part, or in the Section itself. For example, a general definition of 'local social services authority' is given in Section 145(1), but a more limited definition is given in Section 117(3) where the particular local social services authority on which the duty is placed is indicated.

7   The following interpretations are particularly important:
a.   **'Hospital'** The definition of hospital in the Act covers all hospitals in the National Health Service (including Special Hospitals) and any accommodation provided by a local authority and used as a hospital under the National Health Service Act 1977. Any such hospital may admit and detain patients under the procedures laid down in the Act; patients can also be detained in mental nursing homes if the homes are registered for that purpose under the Registered Homes Act 1984.
b.   **'The Managers'** In relation to National Health Service hospitals 'the managers' means the health authority which administers the hospitals; for special hospitals it means the Secretary of State and for mental nursing homes it means the person or persons registered as manager under the Registered Homes Act 1984 (see para 62).

c. **'The responsible medical officer'** The rmo is defined in Section 34(1) as the registered medical practitioner in charge of a detained patient's treatment. In relation to guardianship the rmo is the registered medical practitioner authorised by the responsible local social services authority to act as rmo, for a specific purpose or generally (see para 66).

d. **'The nearest relative'** The terms 'relative' and 'nearest relative' are defined in Section 26 (see para 68 below).

e. **'Approved social workers'** The functions given under the Act to approved social workers may only be carried out by officers of local social service authorities approved for this purpose.

f. **'patient'** A patient is a person suffering from or appearing to suffer from mental disorder (there is a different interpretation of patient in Part VII of the Act, see Section 94).

g. **'treatment'** Treatment is defined as including 'nursing . . . care, habilitation and rehabilitation under medical supervision'.

Part I   Application of Act

Application of the Act (*Section 1*)

8   The Act concerns 'the reception, care and treatment of mentally disordered patients, the management of their property and other related matters' (Section 1(1)). The definition of 'mental disorder' is unchanged from the 1959 Act and it 'means mental illness, arrested or incomplete development of mind, psychopathic disorder and any other disorder or disability of mind'.

Definitions of mental illness, mental impairment, severe mental impairment and psychopathic disorder

9   For most purposes of the Act – which are more fully set out below – it is not enough for a patient to be suffering from any mental disorder as defined above; he must be suffering from one of the four specific categories of mental disorder set out in the Act – mental illness, mental impairment, severe mental impairment or psychopathic disorder.

10   The term **'mental illness'** is undefined, and its operational definition and usage is a matter for clinical judgement in each case. The terms **'mental impairment'** and **'severe mental impairment'** are used in the Act for those cases of mental handicap which are associated with abnormally aggressive or seriously irresponsible conduct. They replaced the terms 'subnormality' and 'severe subnormality' in the 1959 Act and are more narrowly defined. The new terms were intended to distinguish the small minority of mentally handicapped people who need to be detained in hospital or received into guardianship, from the great majority who do not.

11   The definition of 'mental impairment' has two main components. First, it refers to 'a state of arrested or incomplete development of mind which includes significant impairment of intelligence and social functioning'. Secondly there is the qualification that the mental handicap must be associated with abnormally aggressive or seriously irresponsible conduct. This is

intended to ensure that mentally handicapped people are not subject to long term compulsory powers unless the behaviour which is part of their condition in that particular case justifies the use of those powers.

12   The distinction between 'severe mental impairment' and 'mental impairment' is one of degree: the impairment of intelligence and social functioning is 'severe' in the former and only 'significant' in the latter. Slight impairment cannot fall within either definition. The assessment of the level of impairment is a matter for clinical judgement. The responsible medical officer of a detained patient has a continuing responsibility to consider whether a patient still falls within the classification under which he was admitted to hospital (Section 16). This distinction between the two degrees of mental impairment is important because there are differences in the grounds on which patients can be detained, or have their detention renewed if they suffer from severe mental impairment as opposed to mental impairment (paragraphs 19, 71, 99, 123, 130, 131, 140, 170, 178, 181 and 215 below).

13   The definition of psychopathic disorder was therefore revised from the 1959 Act to refer to 'whether or not including significant impairment of intelligence' rather than 'subnormality of intelligence'. As in the 1959 Act, psychopathic disorder must be a **persistent** disorder or disability; in other words there must have been signs that the disorder has existed for a considerable period before a patient can be classified as having psychopathic disorder. It must also result in abnormally aggressive or seriously irresponsible conduct.

14   As with mental impairment the **treatability** of the condition is not mentioned in the definition. However, the effect of Sections 3, 37 and 47 are that those with psychopathic disorder (or mental impairment) cannot be compulsorily admitted to hospital for treatment unless it can be stated that medical treatment is likely to alleviate or prevent a deterioration of their condition. This proviso is more stringent than the inclusion of the words 'Requires or is susceptible to treatment' in the definition of psychopathic disorder and subnormality in the 1959 Act.

15   There may be some cases where it is not immediately clear whether a patient should be classified as suffering from psychopathic disorder or mental impairment/severe mental impairment. For example, if a patient is highly aggressive and this is felt to be primarily a function of a disorder of personality rather than any associated mental handicap, the patient should be classified as suffering from psychopathic disorder. If a patient's aggressive or irresponsible behaviour is felt to be primarily a function of his mental

handicap he should probably be classified as suffering from mental impairment or severe mental impairment. This will of course be a matter for clinical judgement.

Exclusions from the definitions of mental disorder

16   Section 1(3) of the Act states that a person may not be dealt with under the Act as suffering from mental disorder purely by reason of promiscuity, other immoral conduct, sexual deviance or dependence on alcohol or drugs. This means that there are no grounds for detaining a person in hospital because of alcohol or drug abuse alone, but it is recognized that alcohol or drug abuse may be accompanied by or associated with mental disorder. It is therefore possible to detain a person who is dependent on alcohol or drugs if he or she is suffering from a mental disorder arising from or suspected to arise from alcohol or drug dependence or from the withdrawal of alcohol or a drug, if all the other relevant conditions are met. Similarly sexual deviancy is not of itself a mental disorder, for the purposes of the Act, which can provide grounds for compulsory detention.

Part II Admission procedures

Introduction

17   Part II of the Act deals with the circumstances in which, and procedures through which, patients may be compulsorily admitted to and detained in hospital or received into guardianship, otherwise than through the Courts, or on transfer from prison or other institutions (Part III) or on return to the United Kingdom (Part VI).

Admission for assessment (*Section 2*)

18   The term 'assessment', which replaced 'observation' in the 1959 Act, carries the wider connotation of active evaluation which is more in keeping with current professional practice. Admission to and detention in hospital for assessment under Section 2 may be authorised where a patient is (*a*) suffering from mental disorder of a nature or degree which warrants the detention of the patient in hospital for assessment (or for assessment followed by medical treatment) for at least a limited period and (*b*) he ought to be so detained in the interests of his health or safety, or with a view to the protection of others. Detention is for up to 28 days. The words in brackets make it clear that a patient detained under Section 2 may be given treatment other than assessment procedures (but see paragraphs 189 to 205 below on consent to treatment). It is envisaged that many patients will complete their treatment in hospital within a period of detention under section 2 and can then be discharged. Others may stay as informal patients or, if they satisfy the conditions, they can be detained under Section 3 for longer term treatment.

Admission for treatment (*Section 3*)

19   The grounds for admission for treatment are first that the patient is suffering from one or more of the four forms of mental disorder set out in

Part I of the Act – mental illness, mental impairment, severe mental impairment and psychopathic disorder (see paragraphs 9 to 16 above). A patient who is suffering from any other disorder or disability of mind cannot be detained for treatment under this Section. Secondly, the mental disorder must be of a nature or degree which makes it appropriate for the patient to receive medical treatment in hospital. A person may meet one of the definitions of the four forms of mental disorder and yet not be in need of medical treatment in a hospital because he can be treated in the community or under guardianship. Thirdly, for a patient suffering from psychopathic disorder or mental impairment there is an additional condition that medical treatment is likely to alleviate or prevent a deterioration in the patient's condition. Treatment need not be expected to cure the patient's disorder: the condition is satisfied if, in the opinion of the doctors making the medical recommendations, medical treatment is likely to enable the patient to cope more satisfactorily with his disorder or its symptoms, or if it stops his condition from becoming worse. Because the interpretation of medical treatment is a wide one, this condition would be satisfied if, for example, a psychopathic or mentally impaired patient would benefit from care, habilitation or rehabilitation under medical supervision in a hospital. Fourthly, it must be necessary for the health or safety of the patient or for the protection of others that he should receive this treatment, and it cannot be provided unless he is detained (ie he is unwilling to stay as an informal patient).

20   It should be noted that there are no age limits for the admission of patients suffering from mental impairment or psychopathic disorder. The age limit imposed by the 1959 Act was felt to be too rigid and better replaced by the more general requirement that the patient should be likely to benefit from treatment.

Applications for admission to hospital

21   Section 11 sets out the general provisions for applications for admission for treatment, assessment or guardianship (dealt with in 43 et seq). An application for admission must be made by either the patient's nearest relative (see paragraph 68 below), or an approved social worker (see paragraph 7(e) above). An application must be addressed to the managers of the hospital to which admission is sought and must state the qualification of the applicant to make the application. An application for admission for assessment or treatment must be accompanied by written recommendations from two medical practitioners. One of these must be approved under section 12(2) of the Act as having special experience in the diagnosis and treatment

of mental disorder. (Circular HSC (IS)18 (for Wales WHSC (IS)9) 'The Mental Health Act 1959: Approval of medical practitioners under Section 28(2) and the exercise by officers of functions under the Act' gives advice to Health Authorities about the approval of such medical practitioners). One of them should, if practicable, know the patient personally.

22   The procedures for making an application and recording an admission are laid down in Regulation 4. Applications must be served by delivering them to an officer of the managers of the hospital to which admission is sought who is authorised to receive it (Regulation 3(2)). This means that in practice the document should normally be delivered to the hospital itself rather than the DHA offices or equivalent.

Applications for admission for assessment under section 2

23   In the case of admission for assessment both medical recommendations must state that, in the opinion of the practitioner, the patient is suffering from mental disorder of a nature or degree which warrants his detention in a hospital for assessment (or for assessment followed by medical treatment) for at least a limited period, and that he ought to be detained in the interests of his own health or safety or for the protection of other persons. A specific diagnosis of the form of mental disorder is not required, as part of the purpose of the 'assessment' may be to determine this. However, the words 'of nature or degree which warrants (his) detention in a hospital' are intended to restrict the use of the section to patients who are thought to be suffering from a form of mental disorder which would justify admission for treatment. The conditions for Section 2 admissions are not quite so stringent as those for Section 3 admissions because assessment may well be used for the purpose of determining whether the more stringent conditions for admission for treatment are met. The forms of application and recommendations for Section 2 are Forms 1–4. One period of detention under Section 2 cannot follow immediately and should not follow closely on another.

Applications for admission for treatment under section 3

24   The medical recommendations for an admission for treatment must state that, in the opinion of both the medical practitioners, the conditions set out in 19 above are satisfied. The particulars must set out the following details which are prescribed in regulations: the form or forms of disorder from which the patient suffers (both medical recommendations must contain one form of disorder in common); the reasons why the patient cannot

suitably be cared for outside of hospital, or be treated as an out-patient, or be admitted as an informal patient; and, in the case of a patient suffering from psychopathic disorder or mental impairment, the reason why treatment is likely to alleviate or prevent a deterioration in his condition. (Form 10 or 11. All other relevant forms are prescribed in Regulation 4).

Medical recommendations

25   The following requirements apply in general to medical recommendations for the purposes of Part II:

i.   Where the two medical practitioners examine the patient separately, not more than five days must have elapsed between the days on which separate examinations took place (Section 12(1)).

ii.   One of the practitioners should be approved for the purposes of Section 12(2).

iii. One of the practitioners should if practicable, have had previous acquaintance with the patient.

iv.   Except in the cases mentioned below, only one medical recommendation may come from a practitioner on the staff of the hospital to which the patient is to be admitted. This does not apply to a patient to be admitted to a mental nursing home or as a private patient in an NHS hospital, when neither recommendation may come from a doctor on the staff. Section 12(6) states that a general practitioner who is employed part-time in a hospital does not count for the purposes of the Section as a practitioner on its staff. This means that medical recommendations can be given by, for example, a full-time consultant psychiatrist and the patient's GP even if the GP happens to work part-time in the hospital in question.

26   For the first time, the 1983 Act made provision for the practical difficulties which may arise in obtaining two medical recommendations in cases of emergency or urgency where it is in the patient's best interests: for example, where there are comparatively few approved doctors in a District. Both medical recommendations may come from medical practitioners on the staff of the hospital concerned, subject to the following conditions (Subsections 3 and 4 of Section 12):

● fulfilling the conditions set out above would cause delay involving serious risk to the health and safety of the patient; and

● one of the two doctors concerned works at the hospital for less than half the time for which he is bound by contract to work for the NHS; and

● where one recommendation is made by a consultant the other may not be made by a doctor who works under him.

Recommendations may only be given by two doctors on the staff of the same hospital if all three of these conditions are satisfied. Usually the recommendations will be from the patient's GP and the consultant who will be his rmo. A medical practitioner, in making any medical recommendation, is responsible for the information which he provides in connection with the application.

Payment of fees to doctors

27 Doctors are sometimes entitled to special fees for conducting an examination with a view to giving a medical recommendation. These fees can be paid by either a local authority or a health authority, and both should be ready to supply a claims form on request. Where payment is made by a local authority the money can be reclaimed by that authority from the relevant health authority. It may be helpful for a named officer of each authority to be given responsibility for examining and certifying any claims that are received and for making payments. The officer would need to be familiar with Section 37 of the Terms and Conditions of Service for hospital doctors.

Admission for asssessment in cases of emergency

28 In exceptional cases it may be necessary to admit a patient for assessment as an emergency without obtaining a second medical recommendation. An emergency application may be made by an approved social worker or by the nearest relative of the patient, and must state that it is of urgent necessity that the patient should be admitted and detained for assessment, and that compliance with the normal procedures would involve undesirable delay. Only one medical recommendation is required but the practitioner concerned must have seen the patient within the previous *24 hours*. Similarly, the applicant must have seen the patient in the previous *24 hours*. New forms for emergency applications and medical recommendations have been prescribed (forms 5–7). The form for the medical recommendation asks for certain information to clarify the circumstances of the emergency, which may be required by hospital managers or the Mental Health Act Commission.

29 The shorter time period, and the provision that only the *nearest* relative can apply, are intended to ensure that the section is only used in genuine emergencies. The recommendation (on form 7) should preferably be given by a practitioner who has had previous acquaintance with the patient. The application is effective for 72 hours in which time a second medical recommendation must be obtained in accordance with the requirements of

Section 12 (with the exception of the requirement as to the time of the second signature). If the second recommendation is received during that period the patient may be detained for 28 days from admission as if originally admitted under Section 2.

Applications in respect of patients already in hospital

30   An application for 'admission' (in other words compulsory detention) under Section 2 or 3 may be made in respect of patients who are already in hospital as informal patients. An informal patient may also be detained for up to 72 hours under Section 5 if the doctor in charge of his treatment reports that an application for admission under Section 2 or 3 ought to be made. This report should be made on form 12 and should be given immediately to an officer authorised to receive such reports on behalf of the managers (para 65). The 72 hour period begins to run from the time the report is furnished.

31   It may occasionally be necessary to make a report under Section 5(2) in respect of a patient who is not in a psychiatric hospital or the psychiatric wing of a general hospital. Where a patient is receiving psychiatric treatment (even though he may also be receiving non-psychiatric treatment) the doctor in charge of the treatment for the purposes of Section 5(2) will be the consultant or senior psychiatrist concerned. But where an in-patient is not receiving psychiatric treatment, the doctor who is in charge of the treatment the patient is receiving would have power to furnish the report. Where such a report is made by a non-psychiatrist, a senior psychiatrist should see the patient as soon as possible to determine whether the patient should be detained further.

32   Section 5(3) provides that the medical practitioner in charge of a patient's treatment may nominate (ie name) one, but only one, other medical practitioner on the staff of the same hospital to act on his behalf under the section, in his absence. Applications under Section 5(2) may be made in respect of an in-patient in any part of any hospital including a general hospital even if he is not being treated for mental disorder at the time. A nurse of the prescribed class may also detain for up to 6 hours under strictly specified circumstances (see below).

Nurse's six hour holding power (Section 5(4))

33   A first level nurse trained in nursing people suffering from mental illness or mental handicap (see the Mental Health (Nurses) Order 1983) may

detain an informal patient **who is already being treated for mental disorder**, for up to six hours, if it appears to him that:

i. the patient is suffering from mental disorder to such a degree that it is necessary for his health or safety, or for the protection of others, for him to be immediately restrained from leaving the hospital; and

ii. it is not practicable to secure the immediate attendance of a medical practitioner for the purpose of furnishing a report under Section 5(2).

34   The holding power starts after the nurse has recorded his opinion on the prescribed form (form 13) and ends either six hours later, or on the earlier arrival of one of the two doctors entitled to make such a report under section 5(2). The doctor is free either to make such a report or to decide not to detain the patient further (which may, for example, include persuading him to stay voluntarily). The written record made by the nurse must be delivered to the hospital managers, or someone authorized to act on their behalf (see paragraph 65 below), as soon as possible either by the nurse or by someone authorized by the nurse. The nurse, or another nurse of the prescribed class, should also take steps to let the managers know as soon as the power has lapsed by delivering form 16 to them in the same way. The six hour holding period counts as part of the 72 hours, if the doctor concerned decides to make a report under Section 5(2).

Duty to inform nearest relative (Section 11)

35   Section 11(3) requires an approved social worker (see 7(e) above) who makes an application for admission for assessment to take whatever steps are practicable to inform the person, if any, appearing to be the patient's nearest relative that the application is about to be or has been made and of the relative's power to discharge the patient. In the case of an application for admission for treatment or for guardianship the approved social worker should try to consult the nearest relative prior to making the application (Section 11(4)). If the nearest relative objects, the approved social worker cannot proceed, but an unreasonable objection by a relative is one of the grounds in Section 29(3) for a court to transfer the powers of the nearest relative to another person. The Act recognises that it may not always be possible for the approved social worker to identify or to contact the nearest relative (see also para 37 below).

Transport of a patient to hospital

36   An application for admission, including the appropriate medical recommendation or recommendations are sufficient authority for the compulsory removal by the applicant or by anyone authorized by him of a

patient to hospital and his detention there. The authority to remove to hospital expires 14 days after the last medical examination for the purposes of a medical recommendation. In the case of an emergency application the period is 24 hours from the medical examination, or the time when the application was made, whichever is earlier. Where it is necessary to provide transport to take the patient to hospital, this comes within the duty of health authorities to provide ambulance services. If the patient is likely to be unwilling to be moved, the applicant should provide the ambulance attendant or escort with written authority. If the patient escapes while being taken to hospital he may be retaken within the 14 days or 24 hour period, whichever applies (see paras 76–80 below, Section 6 and Regulation 9).

Duty of approved social workers to make applications for admission or for guardianship *(Section 13)*

37   Section 13 lays on an approved social worker a duty to make an application for admission (or guardianship, see para 43–7 below) in any case where he considers an application ought to be made and where, after taking into account the views of the relatives and any other relevant circumstances he thinks it necessary and proper to do so. This does not affect the provisions as to consultation with nearest relatives mentioned above (paragraph 35), but, subject to those provisions, and the powers of the nearest relatives, it lays on approved social workers a duty to act when necessary, particularly if relatives are unable or unwilling to do so. The nearest relative may often prefer that the approved social worker should sign an application. Whoever does so, the approved social worker should give relatives any necessary help by providing a form and explaining the procedure. The person making the application must have seen the patient within a period of 14 days ending with the date of signing the application (24 hours for emergency applications for admission for assessment.) (Sections 11(5) and 4(2)).

38   Section 13(2) requires the approved social worker to interview the patient 'in a suitable manner' – i.e. taking account of any hearing or linguistic difficulties the patient may have. He must also satisfy himself that detention in a hospital is the most appropriate way of providing the care and medical treatment the patient needs. He is required to consider 'all the circumstances' of the case: these will include the past history of the patient's mental disorder, his present condition and the social, familial, and personal factors bearing on it, the wishes of the patient and his relatives, and medical opinion. To do this he will need to consult all those professionally involved in the case (for example the doctor or a community psychiatric nurse). In order to assess the available options the approved social worker will have to

inform himself as to the availability and suitability of other means of giving the patient care and medical treatment, such as treatment as an informal patient, day care, out patient treatment, community psychiatric nursing support, crisis intervention centres, primary health care support, local authority social services provision, and support from friends, relatives and voluntary organisations.

39   Section 13(3) provides that an approved social worker may make an application outside the area of the local social services authority he works for. This might be necessary if, for example, two social service authorities shared an 'out of hours' service, or where a patient is admitted informally to a hospital outside his local authority and then needs to be detained. In the latter case it would be desirable for the social worker who knew the patient best to make the application for admission even though the patient is technically the responsibility of the local authority in which the hospital is situated.

40   Section 13(4) enables the nearest relative to require the social services authority in whose area the patient resides to direct an approved social worker to consider applying for a patient's admission to hospital. If he decides not to make the application he must inform the relative of his reasons in writing.

Social report *(Section 14)*

41   Section 14 provides that when a patient is compulsorily admitted to hospital following an application by his nearest relative, the managers must inform the local social services authority in the area where the patient lived before admission. As soon as practicable the authority must then arrange for a social worker to provide a report on the patient's social circumstances which should be sent to the hospital managers. (This should cover the social aspect of the ground outlined in 38 above.)

Medical examination of the patient after admission

42   There is no statutory provision for a medical examination after admission, but the rmo should examine the patient shortly after admission. If he is not satisfied that the patient should be detained he should discharge him. If he is of the opinion that the patient needs to be detained, but is suffering from a different form or forms of mental disorder to those shown on the application form, he may reclassify him (para 69).

Guardianship

43 Placing a mentally disordered person under guardianship enables the guardian to exercise certain powers which are set out in Section 8. The guardian may be the local social services authority, or an individual approved by the local social services authority, such as a relative of the patient. In almost all cases it should be possible for patients for whom care in the community is appropriate to receive that care without being subjected to the control of guardianship. However, in a small minority of cases guardianship enables a relative or social worker to help a mentally disordered person to manage in his own home or a hostel, where the alternative would be admission to hospital.

44 Patients may only be received into guardianship if they have reached the age of 16 years (para 306). Local authorities have a duty under Section 1 of the Child Care Act 1980 to promote the welfare of children. Children and young people aged under 17 (for whom guardianship might have been used under the 1959 Act) may, in appropriate circumstances, be taken into care by a local social services authority under Section 2 of the Child Care Act 1980 or be made subject to a care order or a supervision order under Section 1 of the Children and Young Persons Act 1969. These powers are considered more appropriate than guardianship to ensure that mentally disordered children receive the care and protection they need, although mental disorder itself is not a ground for taking a child into care or making a care or supervision order. All these options, and guardianship, are open for a child aged 16 years.

The grounds for guardianship

45 The grounds for guardianship are that the patient is suffering from mental illness, mental impairment, severe mental impairment or psychopathic disorder and guardianship must be necessary 'in the interests of the welfare of the patient or for the protection of other persons'. The purpose of guardianship is therefore primarily to ensure that the patient receives care and protection rather than medical treatment, although the guardian does have powers to require the patient to attend for medical treatment (but not to make him accept treatment). A guardianship application must be founded on two medical recommendations, the procedure being similar to an application for admission for treatment (paragraph 19 et seq) (Regulation 5, forms 17–20).

Powers of a guardian

46   The effect of a guardianship application, if accepted, is to give the guardian three specific powers as set down in Section 8(1). The first power is to require the patient to live at the place specified by the guardian. This may be used to discourage the patient from sleeping rough or living with people who may exploit or mistreat him, or to ensure that he resides in a particular hostel or other facility. The second power enables the guardian to require the patient to attend specified places at specified times for medical treatment, occupation, education or training. These might include local authority day centres, an adult training centre, or a hospital, surgery or clinic. The third power enables the guardian to require access to the patient to be given at the place where the patient is living, to any doctor, approved social worker, or other person specified by the guardian. This power could be used, for example, to ensure that the patient did not neglect himself. Section 18 provides that if without his guardian's consent, a patient leaves the place where he is required by his guardian to live, he may be taken into custody and returned within 28 days of leaving. A patient under guardianship may also be transferred to hospital (see para 91–92 below).

Applications for guardianship

47   The applications and recommendations for reception into guardianship must be forwarded to the local social services authority named as the proposed guardian, or to the local social services authority in whose area the proposed guardian lives. The guardianship application, and the guardian, if a private individual, must be accepted by this authority. Form 21 should be used to record acceptance and this form should be attached to the application (Regulation 5(3)). Similarly, the receipt of medical recommendations must be recorded on form 15. If the application is accepted the authority will become 'The responsible local social services authority' (Section 34(3)) holding the power of discharge under Section 23 and with duties of visiting and supervision under Regulation 13. When the guardian is a private individual it will no doubt be usual for the patient to live with him or near to him, but if the patient lives temporarily or permanently in another area, the responsible social services authority is the authority in whose area the guardian lives. Similarly, where a local social services authority is the guardian, it may arrange for the patient to live, temporarily or permanently, outside its own area, but so long as that authority remains guardian it remains responsible for visiting and supervision. In such cases the authority may of course make arrangements with another authority or organisation

for visits to the patient and reports on his welfare to be made by their officers acting on behalf of the responsible social services authority.

48   If the proposed guardian is not the local social services authority, the application should be accompanied by a written statement from the proposed guardian that he is willing to act as guardian (to be set out in Part II of form 17 or 18). The application does not take effect until it is accepted by the local social services authority. When accepted it confers the powers and duties of guardian on the guardian from the date of acceptance. The local social services authority should consider the suitability of any proposed guardian before accepting the application. Any guardian should be a person who can appreciate the special disabilities and needs of a mentally disordered person and who will look after the patient in an appropriate and sympathetic way. The guardian should display an interest in promoting the patient's physical and mental health and in providing for his occupation, training, employment, recreation and general welfare in a suitable way. The local social services authority must satisfy itself that the proposed guardian is capable of carrying out his functions and should assist the guardian with advice and other facilities. Regulation 12 provides that they can call for reports and information from the guardian, as they may require; the guardian also has a duty to inform them of his address, the address of the patient and of the nominated medical attendant, and if the patient should die.

Nominated medical attendant

49   Regulation 12 requires the guardian, if not a local social services authority, to appoint a doctor to act as the 'nominated medical attendant' who will care for the patient's general health. This doctor has the power to reclassify the patient (Section 16) and is responsible for examining the patient when the authority for his guardianship is due to expire and for making a report that the guardianship should be renewed, if appropriate (Section 20). It is for the guardian to decide who to appoint as the nominated medical attendant, but this should be done after consultation with the local social services authority. He may be the patient's general practitioner. When the guardian is a social services authority these functions are carried out by the rmo defined in para 7(c) above. The rmo has the power of discharge in all cases (see para 108 below). It is for the local social services authority to decide who is to act as the rmo, either generally for a particular patient, or on a specific occasion. The responsible local social services authority should wherever practicable nominate a consultant psychiatrist who has been involved in the patient's treatment.

18

Scrutiny and rectification of documents

50 The people who sign the applications and make the medical recommendations should make sure that they comply with the requirements of
the Act. Those who act on the authority of these documents should also
make sure that they are in the proper form, as an incorrectly completed form
may not constitute authority for a patient's detention. Section 15 of the Act
contains provisions under which documents which are found to be incorrect,
defective or insufficient may be rectified after they have been acted on.
Patients may continue to be detained for a limited period while an error
capable of rectification is corrected.

Faulty applications

51 Admission documents should be carefully scrutinised as soon as the
patient has been admitted, or, if he is already in hospital, as soon as the
documents are received. The managers of the hospital should nominate an
officer to undertake this task (para 64, Regulation 4(2)). The following
kinds of faults should be looked for:
a. those which invalidate the application completely and cannot be
   rectified.
b. those which may be amended under Section 15 – in particular those
   which make a medical recommendation insufficient to warrant the
   detention of the patient, but which may be capable of rectification by
   the substitution of a new medical recommendation under Subsections
   (2) and (3) of Section 15.

Faults which invalidate the application

52 Documents cannot be rectified under Section 15 unless they are documents which can properly be regarded as applications or medical
recommendations within the meaning of the Act. A document cannot be
regarded as an application or medical recommendation if it is not signed at
all or is signed by a person who is not empowered to do so under the Act.
This means that a check should be made to confirm that an application is
signed by the patient's nearest relative or the acting nearest relative or an
approved social worker; and that each medical recommendation is signed by
a practitioner who is not excluded under Section 12. In doing so the officer
scrutinising the form may take statements at face value; for example, he
need not check that the doctor who states he is a registered medical practitioner *is* registered (Regulation 3(4)). Another fault which would invalidate

19

the application completely would be if the two medical recommendations did not specify at least one form of mental disorder in common (Section 11(6)).

53   If any fault of this sort is discovered there is no authority for the patient's detention. Authority can only be obtained through a new application. If the patient is already in hospital he can only be detained if the medical practitioner in charge of his treatment (or his nominee) issues a report under Section 5 of the Act. Any new application must, of course, be accompanied by medical recommendations which comply with the Act, but this does not exclude the possibility of one of the two existing medical recommendations being used if the time limits and other provisions of the Act can still be complied with (Sections 11, 12 and 6).

Errors which may be amended under Section 15

54   Section 15 allows an application or medical recommendation which is found to be in any respect incorrect or defective to be amended by the person who signed it, with the consent of the managers of the hospital, within the period of 14 days from the date of the patient's admission. Faults which may be capable of amendment under this section include the leaving blank of any spaces on the form which should have been filled in (other than the signature) or failure to delete one or more alternatives in places where only one can be correct. The patient's forenames and surname should agree in all the places where they appear in the application and supporting recommendations.

55   Any document found to contain faults of this sort should be returned to the person who signed it for amendment. When the amended document is returned to the hospital it should again be scrutinised to check that it is now in the proper form. Consent to the amendment should then be given by a senior officer of the hospital or mental nursing home who has been authorised to consent to amendments on behalf of the managers (Regulation 4(2)). In the case of mental nursing homes, the managers, if two or more in number, may authorise one of their number to consent to amendments. These officers can also issue notices under section 15(2). Similarly, a local social services authority may authorise in writing an officer or class of officers to carry out these functions (Regulation 5(2)). The consent should be recorded in writing and could take the form of an endorsement on the document itself. If this is all done within a period of 14 days starting with the date on which the patient was admitted (or the date when the documents were received if the patient was already in hospital when the application was

made) the documents are deemed to have had effect as though originally made as amended.

Time limits for medical recommendations

56 Another point which should be checked as soon as the documents are first received is whether the time limits mentioned in Sections 11, 12 and 6 have been complied with. Except for emergency applications under Section 4, these limits are:

a. the date on which the applicant last saw the patient must be within the period of 14 days ending with the date of the application.
b. the dates of the medical *examinations* of the patient by the two doctors who gave the recommendations (not the dates of the recommendations themselves) must be not more than 5 clear days apart (ie if one examination took place on 1 January the other can take place no later than 7 January).
c. the dates of signatures of both medical recommendations must not be later than the date of the application.
d. the patient's admission to hospital (or if the patient is already in hospital, the reception of the documents by a person authorised by the hospital managers to receive them) must take place within 14 days beginning with the date of the later of the two medical examinations.

57 When an emergency application is made under Section 4 it is accompanied in the first place by only one medical recommendation. The time limits which apply to emergency applications are:

a. the time at which the applicant last saw the patient must be within the period of 24 hours ending with the time of the application.
b. the patient's admission to hospital must take place within the period of 24 hours starting with the time of the medical examination or with the time of the application whichever is earlier. An emergency application may be signed either before or after the medical recommendation.
c. the second medical recommendation must be received on behalf of the managers not more than 72 hours after the time of the patient's admission. The two medical recommendations must then comply with all the normal requirements except the requirement as to the time of the signature of the second recommendation.

Faulty medical recommendations

58 If the dates entered on the application and medical recommendations do not conform with these time limits, the persons who signed them should

be asked whether the dates or times entered are correct. If they are not correct and the correct dates or times do conform with the limits the entry on the forms may be amended under Section 15(1). If the time limits have not been complied with, then the application is invalid, unless it is capable of rectification by the substituting of a new medical recommendation under Section 15(3).

59   It will be noted that notice of the rejection of a recommendation under Section 15(2) must be sent in writing to the applicant (whereas a request for amendment under Section 15(1) should be sent direct to the person who signed the document in question). It would be advisable at the same time to inform the doctor who gave the recommendation. The applicant – especially when not an approved social worker – should be advised that he may submit a fresh recommendation within the 14 days from the patient's admission. In some cases it may be suitable for the fresh recommendation to be given by a doctor on the staff of the hospital.

60   Section 15(3) allows the procedure described in subsection (2) to be used when both recommendations are good in themselves but taken together are insufficient, eg when neither is given by a doctor approved under Section 12, or when the time limits applying to medical examinations mentioned in paragraphs 56–57 above have not been complied with. In such case either recommendation may be replaced by a fresh one under Section 15(2). But this procedure may not be used if the recommendations do not comply with the requirement in Section 12 that they must agree in specifying at least one form of mental disorder in common, as mentioned in paragraph 52 above.

Approved medical practitioners

61   Another point to be checked in all cases is whether one of the two medical recommendations is given by a practitioner who is approved by the Secretary of State under Section 12(2). Each doctor is required to state in the medical recommendation whether or not he is so approved. The statement can be taken at face value if there is no reason to suspect falsification, but if neither recommendation states that the doctor is approved, enquiries should be made. If in fact one of these doctors is approved, the statement or the recommendation may be amended under Section 15. If neither doctor is approved, but the recommendations are otherwise in proper form, a new recommendation must be sought under Section 15(3).

The managers of hospitals

62   The definition of the 'managers' of a hospital or mental nursing home is covered in paragraph 7(b) above. The power to detain patients admitted under the Act rests with the managers (Section 6(2) and Section 40(1)) and they, amongst others, have powers of discharge (Section 23(2) and 23(3)). Various reports and notices must be given to them, and they have other powers and duties which are described elsewhere in this memorandum. In particular, they have responsibilities for the referral of certain cases to a Mental Health Review Tribunal (Section 68) (Paras 209 and 220) and for withholding patients' correspondence in certain cases (Section 134) (Paras 279 to 285). They must also ensure that patients, and where possible their nearest relatives, are informed of their rights (Section 132), (Paras 274 to 277) and that the nearest relative is informed of a patient's discharge (Section 133) (Para 278). The managers should also be prepared to see patients and their relatives who wish to see them to discuss the possibility of discharge, if they are still dissatisfied after discussions with the rmo. Such interviews should be arranged with as little delay as possible. All the functions mentioned above may be performed on behalf of the managers by members or officers where authorised to do so in accordance with the Act and Regulations.

63   There are specific provisions with regard to the discharge of patients. Section 23(4) allows the manager's power of discharge to be exercised by any three or more members (*not* officers) authorised by them to do so, or by three or more members of a committee or sub-committee of the authority or body they constitute. Health authorities will probably want to authorise all or a large number of their members. The same members will be asked to consider reports reviewing the authority for detention under Section 20. Health authorities can also discharge a patient maintained under contract in a mental nursing home.

Authorised officers

64   Regulation 3(6) permits the delegation to individual officers or to a class of officers the function of making records or reports under the Act. Regulation 4(2) similarly permits the delegation of functions relating to the rectification of documents. The authorisation of officers to perform the functions covered by Regulations 3(6) and 4(2) should be by a resolution of the health authority. It will probably be convenient to authorise all officers holding certain types of posts.

Delivery of documents

65   Regulation 3 provides that any document, other than an application for admission, which is to be delivered to the managers, may either be sent by post or delivered personally to the managers or to any person authorised by them to receive documents on their behalf. These documents include the medical recommendations which constitute the authority for a patient's detention; a report under Section 5 which authorises the detention of a patient not previously liable to be detained; a report by the responsible medical officer which renews the authority for detention under Section 20; and an order for the discharge of a patient, or a notice of intention to make such an order given by the nearest relative under Section 23 or 25; and the written record of the nurse's 6 hour holding power under Section 5. These documents will often either be delivered by hand, or signed on the hospital premises, and an application for admission must be delivered by hand; in any case documents do not take effect until delivered to the person authorised to receive them. (The only exception to this is where the nurse has exercised his holding power, see para 34.) Some of the documents, particularly reports under Section 5 and emergency applications under Section 4 may need to be received outside normal office hours. A patient's relative may wish to hand a notice of intention to discharge the patient to a nurse or social worker when visiting the hospital. The managers should ensure that suitable officers or classes of officers are authorised to receive documents, bearing these circumstances in mind.

The responsible medical officer (rmo)

66   The definition of rmo is covered in 7(c) above. The rmo has certain powers and duties under Parts II and III of the Act including the power to grant leave of absence (para 72); of discharge (para 104); to make a report preventing discharge by the nearest relative (para 104); and to make a report which renews the authority for detention (para 98). All hospital patients should be under the care of a consultant who is in charge in the sense that he is not responsible or answerable for the patient's treatment to any other doctor. It is this doctor who will normally exercise the functions of the responsible medical officer. The examinations and reports authorising renewal under Section 20 can be made at any time during a two month period, and these should normally be undertaken by the patient's usual doctor. But, there are other functions under the Act requiring swift action (eg the decision whether to issue a report barring discharge by the nearest relative under Section 25) and the patient's usual doctor may not be available (eg owing to sickness or absence on annual leave). In that case the

doctor who is for the time being in charge of the patient's treatment (who should normally be another consultant) should exercise the functions of the rmo, although for Section 5 applications it must be the nominated medical practitioner (Section 5(3)) who does so.

The nearest relative *(Sections 26–30)*

67 Various functions are conferred on the patient's nearest relative in connection with applications for admission and discharge, and applications to a Mental Health Review Tribunal. It is open to the nearest relative to authorise some other person under Regulation 14 to perform his functions under the Act. Such authorisation may be given at any time, whether a question of admission to hospital or guardianship has already arisen or not, and it may be revoked at any time. It lapses on the death of the person who made it. While in force it confers the functions of the nearest relative on the person authorised to the exclusion of the person initially defined as nearest relative. The functions of the nearest relative may also be removed from the nearest relative as defined and conferred on some other person by a county court (Sections 29 and 30, see paras 109–114).

68 The nearest relative is defined in Section 26. If a patient has two relatives of equal standing (for example, father and mother), the elder takes precedence. If the patient is usually living with, or cared for by one or more relatives, or persons acting as such, they will take precedence over others. The definition of husband or wife includes a person with whom the patient has been living as a husband or wife for not less than 6 months although such a person does not take precedence over a legal spouse unless there has been a separation or desertion. A person of either sex who has resided with the patient for 5 years or more is also counted as a relative, although he or she comes last in the list. The exclusion under the 1959 Act of a nearest relative who is ordinarily resident abroad, is amended to apply only where the patient is ordinarily resident in the UK.

Reclassification of the patient's disorder

69 Section 16 provides for the reclassification of a patient who is detained for treatment under Section 3 or is subject to guardianship under Section 7. If it appears to the appropriate medical officer (rmo or nominated medical attendant) that a patient is suffering from a different form of mental disorder from the one or more forms specified on the application he may report that to the hospital managers or guardian on form 22 or 23. The report may name

an additional form of disorder which exists together with the other or it can replace the previously recorded form with another. The original application then has effect as if the new form of mental disorder were recorded on it. The nearest relative and the patient must be informed of the reclassification and either of them may then apply to a Mental Health Review Tribunal within 28 days (Section 66).

70 A case requiring reclassification could arise, for example, where a patient with an underlying psychopathic disorder was admitted for the treatment of an episode of mental illness. If the treatment of the mental illness were successful, but the psychopathic disorder remained, the rmo might want to reclassify the disorder from mental illness to psychopathic disorder. If so, he would have to consider whether further treatment in hospital was likely to alleviate or prevent a deterioration of the patient's psychopathic disorder (and whether the other conditions for detention were still satisfied).

71 Section 16(2) ensures that a patient who is reclassified as suffering from psychopathic disorder or mental impairment (but not from mental illness or severe mental impairment) does not continue to be detained in hospital unless the disorder is treatable. In these cases, the rmo must include in his report a statement of his opinion as to whether continued medical treatment in hospital is likely to alleviate or prevent a deterioration in the patient's condition.

Leave of absence from hospital

72 Section 17(1) provides that the rmo may grant a patient leave to be absent from the hospital in which he is liable to be detained, subject to any conditions the rmo thinks necessary in the interests of the patient, or for the protection of other people. Leave of absence can be given either for a temporary absence, or on a specific occasion, after which the patient is expected to return to hospital, or as a period of trial of the patient's suitability for discharge. Leave can be extended in the absence of the patient (Section 17(2)).

73 Section 17(3) states explicitly that the rmo may direct that the patient must remain in custody during his leave if it is necessary in the interests of the patient or for the protection of other persons. The patient may be kept in the custody of an officer on the staff of the hospital or of any other person authorised in writing by the managers of the hospital. These kinds of arrangement would allow detained patients to have escorted leave for outings, to attend other hospitals for treatment, or to have home visits on

compassionate grounds. If a patient is granted leave of absence on condition that he stays in another hospital, he may be kept in the custody of any officer on the staff of the other hospital. This kind of arrangement can be made for a trial period before a formal transfer from one hospital to another (see para 82).

Recall from leave

74   If a patient is on leave and it appears to the rmo that it is necessary to recall the patient to hospital in the interests of the patient's health and safety or for the protection of other persons, he may do so by giving notice to the patient or the person in charge of the patient during his leave (Section 17(4)). A patient cannot be recalled if the period of his detention has lapsed; or if he has had six months continuous leave without returning to hospital or being transferred to another hospital, unless he is absent without leave at the end of the six months (Section 17(5)).

Leave as trial for discharge

75   When a patient is sent on leave as a trial for discharge any necessary initial arrangements for somewhere for him to live and a job or day centre placement should normally be made by, or in consultation with, the local social services authority and after discussion with his nearest relative, if practicable. The local authority's social workers, who are likely to be involved in his aftercare, may be responsible for visiting him on leave; it may also be helpful for him to receive support from community psychiatric nurses, and if appropriate this should be arranged with the local DHA.

Absence without leave

76   Section 18 provides powers for retaking patients who are absent without leave from hospital, or from the place where they are required to live (by the conditions of their leave or by their guardian), or who fail to return from leave either at the end of leave or when recalled. A patient who is liable to be detained in a hospital may be retaken by any approved social worker, any officer on the staff of the hospital where he is liable to be detained (but see para 77), any person authorised in writing by the managers of the hospital where the patient is liable to be detained, or any constable (see paras 288–293). A patient who is absent without leave while under guardianship may be taken into custody by any officer on the staff of a local social services

27

authority, any constable, or any person authorised in writing by the guardian or a local social services authority (Section 18(3)).

77 Section 18(2) provides for the return of patients who go missing while on leave of absence. If such a patient is, as a condition of his leave, required to reside in a hospital other than the one in which he is formally liable to be detained, he may be taken into custody by a member of staff of the hospital where he is on leave, or anyone authorised by the managers of that hospital.

Time limits for retaking patients absent without leave

78 If a patient remains out of custody for 28 days he cannot be retaken under Section 18 (see subsection 4 of that section) and a fresh application for treatment or guardianship would have to be made if compulsory powers were still appropriate. Section 18(5) states that a patient cannot be taken into custody under section 18 if the period of his detention under one of the following short-term powers has expired: admission for assessment (section 2(4)), emergency admission (Section 4(4)), the detention of an in-patient by his doctor (Section 5(2)) or by a nurse (Section 5(4)). This time limit applies to all forms of mental disorder.

Powers for retaking patients in any part of the UK, Channel Islands or Isle of Man

79 Section 88 permits patients who are absent without leave from hospitals (but not from the place where they are required to live by a guardian) in England and Wales to be retaken in any other part of the United Kingdom, the Channel Islands or the Isle of Man. Patients can be retaken in these places by anyone who has power to retake them in England and Wales under Section 18 or by the equivalent to approved social workers in Scotland or Northern Ireland (see Section 88(3)) or by the police of the country where they are found.

Special provisions as to patients absent without leave

80 Section 21 provides that where a patient is absent without leave, he remains liable to be detained (or subject to guardianship) until the end of the period mentioned in para 78 above, or the day on which he is returned or returns to hospital, whichever is the earlier, but, if he does return his detention or guardianship is extended by a week if less than a week is left before the authority would expire. This allows time for the rmo to examine

the patient and decide whether he wishes to make a report under section 20(3) or 20(6). If he does, the renewal takes effect from the day on which the authority would have expired apart from Section 21.

Transfer of patients

81 Sections 19 and 123 of the Act and regulations 7 and 8 define the circumstances in which patients who are liable to be detained or who are under guardianship may be transferred between hospitals or guardians or between hospital and guardianship, and lay down the procedures to be followed. Section 10 makes separate provision for the death or incapacity of a guardian or circumstances when the guardian wishes to relinquish guardianship or if he has performed his functions negligently or in a manner contrary to the interests of the welfare of the patient.

Transfer of patients detained in hospital

82 The hospital in which the patient is liable to be detained is named in the application for admission. Section 19(3) allows a patient to be detained in any other hospital administered by the same managers. Section 123(1) permits the Secretary of State to direct a patient's transfer from one special hospital to another, and section 123(2) permits him to direct the transfer of a special hospital patient to a hospital which is not a special hospital.

83 If it is decided that a detained patient needs to go to another hospital which is not under the same managers, it may be possible to send him there on leave under Section 17, as long as the period does not exceed 6 months. The power to detain and discharge would then remain with the managers and the rmo at the first hospital, who would also have the power to recall the patient to that hospital (but see para 77).

Transfer to and from another hospital or special hospital

84 If a patient is to remain more than six months in another hospital he should be formally transferred under Section 19 using the procedure laid down in Regulation 7, unless he can be discharged and can continue as an informal patient. The formal authority for transfer (form 24) should not be signed until the arrangements for the transfer have been finalised. If transfer to a special hospital is thought necessary, the Department of Health and Social Security, which controls all admissions to special hospitals, must be approached (see paras 266–271). The authority for transfer is given by the

managers of the transferring hospital (Regulation 7). District, and where relevant special, health authorities will probably wish to give a general authority to senior administrative and medical officers to authorise transfers. The authority to detain, and the power of discharge, are transferred to the managers and the rmo at the new hospital from the date on which the patient is admitted, or if the patient is already at the new hospital on leave, from the date on which the transfer authority is received. The authority for transfer is valid for 28 days (see Regulation 9). Detention documents must be transferred to the receiving hospital with the authority for transfer (see para 95). In the case of patients detained in mental nursing homes, the patient may be transferred to another mental nursing home under the same management without a formal procedure, but a note of the transfer should be kept with the admission documents (Regulation 7(4)).

Transfer from hospital to guardianship

85   A patient may be transferred to guardianship under the procedure laid down in Regulation 7. The responsible local social services authority should be consulted, their agreement obtained and recorded (in Part II of form 25), and the necessary arrangements made before the authority for transfer (form 25) is sent to them. Where the guardian is a private person, his agreement must also be obtained and recorded in Part III of form 25. The transfer takes effect on the date specified by the local social services authority when they confirm the arrangements for the transfer. Until that date the patient remains liable to be detained but there is no reason why, if he is not already on leave, he should not be given leave under Section 17 to take up residence outside the hospital before the date. Transfers may be authorised in respect of patients detained under either Section 2 or 3. The authority for transfer is valid for 14 days (see Regulation 9).

Need to consult nearest relative about patient's transfer

86   The patient's nearest relative should normally be consulted before a patient is transferred to another hospital or to guardianship, and he should be notified when the transfer has taken place. His consent to the transfer is not a statutory requirement, but he has the power of discharge (para 104 et seq).

Transfer of patients under guardianship

87   Transfer from one guardian to another can take place under Section 10, or, depending on the circumstances, under Section 19. In the latter case the

procedure laid down in Regulation 8 must be followed. If a guardian wishes to give up guardianship he can arrange this by giving notice to the responsible local social services authority (Section 10(1)). Under Section 10 the guardianship passes automatically to the authority if the guardian dies. Guardianship could subsequently be transferred to another individual under Regulation 8 if this were desirable.

88   When guardianship is to be transferred to an individual guardian who has already come forward, or to a local social services authority in another area, the procedure under Regulation 8 applies. The authority for transfer should be given by the existing guardian on form 26. This authority is then subject to confirmation by the responsible local social services authority (to be recorded in Part II of form 26), and takes effect from the date specified by them. Where the guardian is a private person, his agreement must also be obtained and recorded in Part III of form 26. Immediately after the transfer, the new guardian (if an individual) must appoint a nominated medical attendant (paras 48 and 49), and notify the authority of the nominated medical attendant's address and the address at which the patient lives (Regulation 12).

Temporary guardians

89   Section 10(2) allows the responsible local social services authority, or any person authorised by them, to act temporarily on behalf of a guardian who is ill or incapacitated. The authority or person acting as guardian under this subsection acts as an agent for the real guardian and may not go against any wishes or instructions he may express.

Unsatisfactory guardians

90   If the responsible local social services authority considers that the patient should be transferred because the present guardian is unsatisfactory on the grounds mentioned in Section 10(3), an application can be made to the County Court for an order under that subsection, even if the present guardian is unwilling to give up guardianship.

Admissions to hospital of patients under guardianship

91   If a patient under guardianship requires treatment in hospital and there is no need to detain him there, he may be admitted informally. He then

remains under guardianship unless discharged from guardianship or transferred. Guardianship can also remain in force if the patient is admitted to hospital on an application for admission for assessment under Sections 2 or 4. It does not remain in force if the patient is admitted for treatment (Section 6(4)).

Compulsory admission to hospital for treatment of patients under guardianship

92   If it is decided that the patient needs to be detained in hospital for more than 28 days, an application for admission for treatment may be made under Section 3, or more usually he may be transferred under Regulation 8(3). In either of these cases guardianship lapses as soon as the application for admission or the authority for transfer takes effect. The procedure for transfer is similar to the procedure for admission under Section 3, and the application does not take effect until it is accepted by the managers of the hospital to which it is addressed. The responsible local social services authority must take such steps as are practicable to inform the nearest relative of the transfer and consult him in the same way as for an admission under Section 3 (para 35 and Regulation 8(3)). A county court order under Section 29 conferring the functions of the nearest relative on some other person does not expire when a patient is transferred under regulations but it does expire if for any other reason the patient ceases to be liable to detention or subject to guardianship.

Appplications for transfer to hospital from guardianship

93   A transfer to hospital is subject to the conditions set out in Regulation 8(3) and must be authorised by the responsible local social services authority on form 27 and accompanied by an application for admission for treatment (form 9) and two supporting medical recommendations (form 28 or 29). The provisions of Sections 11, 12 and 13 apply to the authority for transfer and the medical recommendations (Regulation 8(3)(a)). In particular, the approved social worker concerned has a duty to consult the nearest relative under Section 11(4). The provisions of Section 15 concerning the rectification of applications and recommendations do not apply to recommendations given in support of a transfer. The application and recommendations should be scrutinised carefully to make sure they comply with the requirements of the Act and Regulations before the authority for transfer is signed.

94   A correctly completed authority for transfer to hospital, together with an application for admission for treatment, is sufficient authority to take the

patient to hospital and detain him there, as long as he is admitted within 14 days beginning with the date of the later of the two medical examinations on which the recommendations are based (see Regulation 9). On the transfer of the patient the managers of the hospital must record his admission on form 14. Guardianship ceases on the date of admission and the patient is then in the same position as any other patient admitted under Section 3. In particular he has the same right to apply to a Mental Health Review Tribunal (this is the effect of Section 19(2)(*d*)).

Documents

95   When a patient is transferred under Section 10 or 19, the documents authorising guardianship or detention, including the authority for transfer, should be sent to the hospital or guardian to which the patient is transferred. The former hospital or guardian should retain copies of these documents.

Expiry or renewal of authority for detention or guardianship

96   Section 20 contains the provisions governing the duration of the authority for the detention for treatment, or guardianship, and its expiry and renewal.

97   The initial authority for detention or guardianship lasts for 6 months, as does the first renewal. Subsequent renewals are for one year. This means that the rmo must review the need for continued detention or guardianship after four months and ten months and then every year. Any patient except one subject to a hospital order (see paras 218–219) has the right to apply to a Mental Health Review Tribunal within the first six months, and again in the second six months if his detention or guardianship is renewed. Subsequent applications may be made once in every 12 month period of detention.

98   Section 20(3) requires the rmo to examine a patient detained for treatment during the two months preceding the day on which the authority for his detention is due to expire. If it appears to the rmo that the patient should continue to be detained the rmo should report that to the hospital managers using form 30 and this report should be kept with the admission documents. Before he makes a report, the rmo must satisfy himself that all the conditions set out in Section 20(4) are satisfied. These conditions, which must be satisfied for the renewal of the authority to detain, are substantially the same as the conditions for admission for treatment, but in the case of a mentally ill or severely mentally impaired patient there is an alternative to one of the conditions.

Conditions for the renewal of detention

99   The first of the conditions for renewal of detention is that the patient is suffering from mental illness, severe mental impairment, psychopathic disorder or mental impairment *and* that the disorder is of a nature or degree which makes it appropriate for him to receive medical treatment in a hospital. This is the same condition as in Section 3(2)(*a*) and it ensures that detention can only continue if the patient is still suffering from one of the four named disorders, and if the disorder is serious enough to make hospital treatment appropriate. The second condition is that hospital treatment is likely to alleviate or prevent a deterioration of the patient's condition. (This is the same as Section 3(2)(*b*) but for the purposes of renewal the condition is applied to all four forms of mental disorder.) Alternatively, **in the case of a patient suffering from mental illness or severe mental impairment**, it is sufficient that the patient, if discharged, is unlikely to be able to care for himself, to obtain the care he needs, or to guard himself against serious exploitation. The third condition is that it is necessary for the health or safety of the patient, or for the protection of others that he should receive medical treatment in a hospital, and that it cannot be provided unless he continues to be detained. This is the same as Section 3(2)(*c*). The last part of this condition means that a patient cannot continue to be detained if he is willing and able to receive treatment as an informal patient.

Conditions for the renewal of guardianship

100   Section 20(6) provides for the renewal of the authority for guardianship. It requires the rmo or nominated medical attendant (Para 49) to examine the patient during the two months before the authority for guardianship expires. If it appears to the doctor that it is necessary in the interests of the welfare of the patient or for the protection of other persons that the patient should remain under guardianship he must report that on form 31 to the local social services authority (or to an officer authorised on their behalf) and to the guardian when he is an individual. Guardianship may only be renewed if the conditions for a guardianship application (Para 45) apply to the renewal as to the original application.

Recording a change in the form of mental disorder

101   Section 20(9) provides for cases where the rmo or nominated medical attendant decides, after examining the patient, that he is suffering from a disorder or form of disorder different from that named on the original

34

application. If a report made under Section 20(3) or (6) names a different form of mental disorder from that named in the application, this has the effect of reclassifying the patient and there is no need for a separate report under Section 16 (Para 69).

Informing the patient of the decision about renewal

102   Sections 20(3) and 20(6) require the hospital managers or local social services authority to inform the patient if they do not discharge him. The managers or local social services authority should consider whether or not to use their powers to discharge the patient (Para 104). The members who are authorised to exercise the power of discharge (Para 63) should therefore consider the renewal report and record their decision at the bottom of the form 30 or 31. A patient need only be interviewed if he requests it or if the managers think it desirable after reading the renewal report.

103   Normally the whole procedure outlined above should be completed within the two month period allowed for the doctor's examination, and the patient should be informed, by the managers, or local social services authority, of their decision no later than the renewal date. If, however, there is any delay it is the renewal report itself which gives the continued authority for detention whether or not it has been considered by the managers; and the patient should in any case be informed of the report before the renewal date. The patient's right to apply to a Mental Health Review Tribunal applies from the date of renewal.

Discharge by rmo, nearest relative or hospital managers

104   In all cases patients admitted for treatment or assessment may be discharged by the rmo, the nearest relative or the hospital managers. Any three or more members of the health authority which manages the hospital, or committee or sub-committee of that authority, may exercise this power if they have been authorised to do so by the authority or a committee or sub-committee (Section 23(4)). The rmo may discharge the patient without reference to the hospital managers. If the nearest relative wishes to discharge the patient he must give the hospital managers not less than 72 hours notice in writing of his intention. There is no prescribed form of notice but there is a form (34) for the nearest relative to use for the order itself if he wishes. The notice and order for discharge must be served either by delivery of the order or notice at the hospital to an officer of the managers authorised by them to receive it, or by sending it by prepaid post to those managers at

that hospital (Regulation 3(3)). If the rmo thinks that, if discharged, the patient is likely to act in a manner dangerous to other persons or himself the rmo may within that 72 hours report his view on form 36 to the hospital managers (Section 25).

105   The effect of such a report is to prevent the nearest relative from discharging the patient then or at any time in the subsequent six months. If this report is issued in respect of a patient detained for treatment, the managers must inform the nearest relative in writing without delay, and should remind him of his right to apply to a Mental Health Review Tribunal within 28 days (Section 66(1)(g) and (2)(d)). In the case of a patient detained for assessment the nearest relative has no right to apply to an MHRT if discharge is barred but the patient himself has the right to apply to a tribunal during the first 14 days of detention, and again if he is subsequently detained for treatment (para 97).

106   Where a patient is detained in a mental nursing home for assessment or treatment he may be discharged by the Secretary of State, and if the patient is maintained in such a home under contract with a health authority, he may be discharged by that authority (Section 23(3)).

107   The nearest relative's written notice of intention to discharge may be delivered in any of the ways described in para 65. The 72 hour period starts to run from the time when the notice is received by an authorised person, or is delivered by post at the hospital to which it is addressed. Therefore all hospitals in which patients are detained should have suitable arrangements for opening post, whether delivered by hand or by the Post Office, at weekends and during holidays. As soon as the notice is received, the time of receipt should be recorded and the rmo should be informed.

Discharge from guardianship by rmo, local social services authority or nearest relative

108   A patient who is subject to guardianship may be discharged by the rmo (Para 7(c)), the responsible local social services authority, or the nearest relative. Discharge by the nearest relative cannot be barred, and is effective when the responsible local social services authority receive the order for discharge. The nearest relative may use form 35 to order discharge if he wishes. The power of discharge can be exercised by three or more members of the local social services authority or of a committee or sub-committee in the same way as it can be exercised by a health authority for the purposes of Section 23 (see 104 above).

Appointment by a court of an acting nearest relative

109   Sections 29 and 30 contain various provisions to enable someone to exercise the functions of the nearest relative of a patient who has no nearest relative in the terms of the Act (Sections 26 to 28, see para 67 et seq), or whose nearest relative is unable to act as such due to illness or mental disorder. Section 29 gives the county court power to make an order directing that the functions of the nearest relative shall be exercised by another person, or by a local social services authority. An application for such an order may be made by any relative of the patient, any other person with whom the patient lives or last lived before entering hospital, or by an approved social worker. The person appointed as acting nearest relative may be the applicant or some other person.

110   There are four grounds for making an order under Section 29, and they are set out in Section 29(3)(a)–(d). Paragraphs (a) and (b) cover circumstances where the patient has no nearest relative as defined in the Act, or where it is not reasonably practicable to identify his nearest relative, or where the nearest relative is too ill or mentally disordered to act as such. In the case where there is no nearest relative there is no obligation to seek an order, but this may be done if someone comes forward who wishes to perform the function of the nearest relative. Section 29(5) provides that an order made on these grounds may specify a period for which the order will remain in force, unless it is discharged. One example of a way in which a court might use this power would be to specify that the order should cease on the date when the eldest child of the patient reached 18, so that he could then take on the role of nearest relative. Paragraphs (c) and (d) relate to cases where the nearest relative has been acting unreasonably in objecting to an application for admission for treatment or for guardianship, or in attempting to discharge the patient. In these cases it will be for the approved social worker who wishes to make the application, in consultation with his superiors, and with the doctors who are prepared to give medical recommendations, to consider whether he should apply for a county court order.

Discharging or varying the court order about the nearest relative

111   Section 30 gives the court power to discharge or vary an order under Section 29, and also specifies the duration of an order which has not been discharged. Section 30(4) means that the order lasts either for the period specified under Section 29(5) or until the patient is discharged from hospital or guardianship if he was detained in hospital for treatment or subject to guardianship at the time the order was made, or became so within the

following three months. However, the order does not lapse in the event of a transfer between hospital and guardianship, or between hospitals or guardians.

112 An application to a county court on the ground that the nearest relative is likely to discharge the patient unreasonably cannot be used to prevent a patient's discharge on the order of the nearest relative. An rmo's report barring discharge should be used for this purpose (104 above). However, a county court order can be used to prevent the power of discharge being used unreasonably a second time. In such cases the staff of the hospital concerned should consult the local social services authority, and if it is decided to apply to a county court, the hospital should provide any necessary evidence to support the application. An application should only be made if it is expected that the patient will be re-admitted within 3 months of the order being made. A displaced relative may apply for the patient's discharge to a Mental Health Review Tribunal during each 12 month period of detention, under Section 66.

113 An application to the county court may be made while the patient is detained for assessment, or he can be admitted for assessment while an application to the court is pending. In such cases the patient may be detained under Section 2 until the county court proceedings are disposed of, including the time for lodging an appeal (which is 21 days after the making of the court's order), and if an appeal is lodged, the time taken to determine it. Once an order is made the patient can be detained for a further 7 days.

114 Where jurisdiction under Sections 10, 29 and 30 of the Act is exercised by the county court, the county court rules, which are made by the County Court Rule Committee, will govern the proceedings.

Part III Powers of the Courts and Home Secretary

Introduction

115 Part III deals with the circumstances in which patients may be admitted to and detained in hospital or received into guardianship on the order of a court, or may be transferred to hospital or guardianship from penal institutions on the direction of the Home Secretary. In addition to the powers of the courts to make hospital or guardianship orders (Section 37), the Act gives the courts three extra powers: remands to hospital for a medical report; remands to hospital for treatment; and interim hospital orders (Sections 35, 36 and 38).

Remand to hospital for report on mental condition

116 Section 35 empowers the courts to order the remand to hospital of an accused person for the preparation of a report on his mental condition. This provides an alternative to remanding the accused person in custody for a medical report, in circumstances where it would not be practicable to obtain the report if he were remanded on bail (for instance because he might decide to break a condition of bail that he should reside at a hospital, and the hospital would then be unable to prevent him from discharging himself).

117 The power applies to the following categories of person:
a. where the power is being exercised by the Crown Court, to any person who is awaiting trial before that court for an offence punishable with imprisonment or who is at any stage of such a trial prior to sentence (other than a person convicted of murder)
b. where the power is being exercised by the magistrates' court, to any person
    i.   convicted of an offence punishable on summary conviction with imprisonment; or
    ii. charged with such an offence, if the court is satisfied that he did the act or made the omission charged or if he has consented to the exercise of the power,

118 The power may be exercised only if:

a. the court is satisfied on the written or oral evidence of a registered medical practitioner, approved by the Secretary of State under Section 12, that there is reason to suspect that the accused person is suffering from mental illness, psychopathic disorder, severe mental impairment or mental impairment; and

b. the court is of the opinion that it would be impracticable for a report on his mental condition to be made if he were remanded on bail; and

c. the court is satisfied, on the written or oral evidence of the registered medical practitioner who would be responsible for making the report or some other person representing the managers of the hospital, that the patient will be admitted to hospital within seven days of the date of remand.

119 Remand is in the first instance for up to 28 days, after which the accused person may be further remanded for periods of up to 28 days, but only:

a. if it appears to the court, on the written or oral evidence of the registered medical practitioner responsible for making the report, that this is necessary for completing the assessment; and

b. up to a maximum total period of 12 weeks.

The power of further remanding the accused person may be exercised by the court in his absence if he is legally represented and his representative is given the opportunity to be heard. The court may terminate the remand at any time: and the accused person is entitled to obtain a separate medical report from a registered medical practitioner of his own choice, and at his own expense, and to apply to the court on the basis of it for his remand to be terminated.

120 The effect of the remand is, first, to direct a constable (or any other person chosen by the court) to convey the accused person to the hospital specified in the order, and, second, to entrust responsibility for his detention and reappearance in court to the managers of the hospital. If the accused person absconds, he may be arrested without warrant by any constable and is then to be brought before the court that remanded him, which may decide on some alternative approach to his case.

Remand to hospital for treatment

121 Section 36 empowers the Crown Court to order the remand to hospital of an accused person for treatment. This provides an alternative to the Home Secretary's power under section 48 to transfer unsentenced prisoners to hospital in an emergency.

122   The power applies to a person who is in custody awaiting trial before the court for an offence punishable with imprisonment (other than murder) or who is in custody at any stage of such a trial prior to sentence.

123   The power may be exercised only if the court is satisfied:

a.   on the written or oral evidence of two registered medical practitioners, one of whom must be approved by the Secretary of State under section 12, that the accused is suffering from *mental illness or severe mental impairment* of a nature or degree which makes it appropriate for him to be detained in hospital for medical treatment; and

b.   on the written or oral evidence of the registered medical practitioner who would be in charge of the accused person's treatment, or of some other person representing the managers of the hospital, that the patient will be admitted to hospital within seven days of the date of remand.

124   Paragraphs 119 and 120 above also apply to remands to hospital for treatment under section 36, with the difference that since the purpose of the remand is the accused person's treatment rather than the preparation of a report on him, further remands depend simply on written or oral evidence from the responsible medical officer that a further remand is warranted (but the patient can still apply for the remand to be terminated on the basis of a medical report he has obtained himself).

Interim hospital orders

125   To assist the courts and the hospitals in determining whether it is appropriate to make a hospital order in respect of an offender, section 38 empowers the courts to make an interim hospital order so that the offender's response in hospital can be evaluated without any irrevocable commitment on either side to this method of dealing with the offender if it should prove unsuitable.

126   The power applies to the same categories of person as do hospital orders (see paragraph 130) but a magistrates' court cannot make an interim hospital order in respect of an unconvicted person.

127   The power may be exercised only if:

a.   the court is satisfied, on the written or oral evidence of two registered medical practitioners, one of whom must be approved by the Secretary of State under section 12, and one of whom must be employed by the hospital to be specified in the order,

   i.   that the offender is suffering from mental illness, psychopathic disorder, severe mental impairment or mental impairment; and

ii. that there is reason to suppose that the mental disorder is such that it may be appropriate for a hospital order to be made in his case; and

b. the court is satisfied, on the written or oral evidence of the registered medical practitioner who would be in charge of the offender's treatment, or of some other person representing the managers of the hospital, that the offender will be admitted within 28 days of the order.

128   An interim hospital order may be made in the first instance for a period of up to 12 weeks, and may be renewed for further periods of up to 28 days to a maximum total period of 6 months. Both the power of renewal, and the power to convert an interim hospital order into a hospital order, may be exercised by the court in the absence of the offender if he is legally represented and his representative is given the opportunity to be heard. The court may also terminate the interim hospital order, after considering the written or oral evidence of the responsible medical officer, and deal with the offender in some other way.

129   The effect of an interim hospital order, is first, to direct a constable (or any other person chosen by the court) to convey the offender to the hospital specified in the order, and, second, to entrust responsibility for his detention and reappearance in court to the managers of the hospital. If the offender absconds, he may be arrested without warrant by any constable and is then to be brought before the court that made the order, which may decide on an alternative way of dealing with him.

Hospital and guardianship orders

130   Section 37 empowers courts to make a hospital or guardianship order in respect of certain categories of offender:

a. where the power is being exercised by the Crown Court, in respect of any person convicted before that court for an offence punishable with imprisonment (other than murder).

b. where the power is being exercised by the magistrates' court; (i) in respect of any person convicted by that court of an offence punishable on summary conviction with imprisonment, and (ii), in respect of any person charged before that court with such an offence who would, if convicted, be liable to be made subject to a hospital or guardianship order as a person suffering from mental illness or severe mental impairment, if the court is satisfied that he did the act or made the omission charged.

131   The power to make a hospital order may be exercised if:

a. the court is satisfied, on the written or oral evidence of two registered medical practitioners, one of whom must be approved by the Secretary of State under section 12:
   i. that the offender is suffering from mental illness, psychopathic disorder, severe mental impairment or mental impairment; and
   ii. that the offender's mental disorder is of a nature or degree which makes it appropriate for him to be detained in a hospital for medical treatment; and
   iii. that in the case of an offender suffering from psychopathic disorder or mental impairment, such treatment is likely to alleviate or prevent a deterioration of his condition; and
b. the court is satisfied, on the written or oral evidence of the registered medical practitioner who would be in charge of the offender's treatment, or of some other person representing the managers of the hospital named in the order, that the offender will be admitted to that hospital within 28 days of the date of the order; and
c. the offender is described by each of the medical practitioners whose evidence is taken into account as suffering from the same form, or one of the same forms, of mental disorder; and
d. the court is of the opinion, having regard to all the circumstances including the nature of the offence and the character and antecedents of the offender, and to the other available methods of dealing with him, that a hospital order is the most suitable method of dealing with the case.

132 The power to make a guardianship order may be exercised if:
a. the court is satisfied, on the written or oral evidence of two registered medical practitioners, one of whom must be approved by the Secretary of State under section 12:
   i. that the offender is suffering from mental illness, psychopathic disorder, severe mental impairment or mental impairment; and
   ii. in the case of an offender who has attained the age of 16 years, the mental disorder is of a nature or degree which warrants his reception into guardianship; and
b. the court is of the opinion, having regard to all the circumstances including the nature of the offence and the character and antecedents of the offender, and to the other available methods of dealing with him that a guardianship order is the most suitable method of dealing with the case.

133 Where a patient is admitted to hospital under a hospital order or

placed under guardianship by a guardianship order, any previous application for admission or guardianship and any previous hospital or guardianship order still in existence ceases to have effect. However, if the later order is subsequently quashed on appeal the previous application or order remains in effect and will validate any period of detention under the later order.

134 The court may not, at the same time as making a hospital or guardianship order in respect of an offender, pass a sentence of imprisonment or youth custody or impose a fine or make a probation order or a supervision order or an order for the offender's parent or guardian to enter into a recognizance to take proper care of and exercise proper control over him; but the court may otherwise make any other order which it has the power to do.

Restriction orders

135 Section 41 empowers the Crown Court (but not magistrates' court), when making a hospital order, to make in addition a restriction order. Orders restricting a discharge may be made under section 41 only when a hospital order is also made, not when a guardianship order is made.

136 The requirements for the making of a restriction order are:
a. that it appears to the court, having regard to:
   i.   the nature of the offence, and
   ii. the antecedents of the offender, and
   iii. the risk of his committing further offences if discharged,
   that a restriction order is necessary for the protection of the public from serious harm; and
b. that at least one of the registered medical practitioners whose evidence is taken into account has given oral evidence to the court.

137 Any restriction order may be either for a specified period or without limit of time and may be terminated at any time by the Home Secretary under section 42(1).

Committal to the Crown Court for a restriction order

138 A magistrates' court has no power to make a restriction order. If such a court is satisfied that the conditions exist in which it could make a hospital order, but also feels that a restriction order should be made in addition, it may commit an offender (if over 14 years old) to the Crown Court, under section 43 of the Act. Section 44 provides that the magistrate may direct his

detention, pending the hearing of the case by the Crown Court, in any hospital to which arrangements have been made to admit him. This will normally be the hospital which had already agreed to admit the patient in the event of the magistrates' court itself making a hospital order.

139 A patient admitted to hospital under Section 44 is to be detained as if he were subject to a hospital order with a restriction order (see paragraphs 160–167) and is to be produced from the hospital to attend the Crown Court. It will be the managers' duty to arrange for his attendance with an appropriate escort. It will not be necessary to obtain the Home Secretary's consent to leave of absence from the hospital for this purpose. If a considerable time elapses between the hearing by the magistrates and the hearing by the Crown Court, the hospital authorities should arrange for two fresh medical reports to be submitted to the court (one by a doctor approved under section 12). They should also arrange for at least one doctor to be available to give oral evidence. After appearing before the Crown Court the patient will not be liable to be taken back to the hospital compulsorily unless that court makes a hospital order.

140 If while the patient is detained under Section 44 his mental condition deteriorates to such an extent that he is unlikely to be fit to appear before the Crown Court on the day of the hearing, the court should be notified immediately. In those circumstances the court may either adjourn the case or, if the patient is suffering from mental illness or severe mental impairment, it may make a hospital order, with or without a restriction order, in his absence under powers conferred by section 51. The court can make a hospital order in the patient's absence only if it is satisfied, on the written or oral evidence of at least two doctors, that the patient is suffering from mental illness or severe mental impairment of a nature or degree which makes it appropriate for the patient to be detained in hospital for medical treatment. In informing the court of a patient's unfitness to appear, the hospital authorities should enquire whether it is likely to wish to proceed in the patient's absence, and if so they should arrange for two doctors, one of whom must be a doctor approved under section 12 of the Act, to attend at the court to give evidence of the patient's mental state.

Medical evidence

141 Courts may make a hospital order or guardianship order or include in a probation order a requirement under section 3 of the Powers of Criminal Courts Act 1973, on the basis of written medical reports, but they may, if they wish, call the doctors to give oral evidence. If a court proposes to make

a restriction order in addition to a hospital order it is required to hear oral evidence from at least one doctor. Medical reports should normally be submitted in writing to the court in advance of the hearing, and the doctors should be prepared to give oral evidence if required. They may be asked to do so at comparatively short notice, especially in the Crown Court.

Arrangements for report on defendants granted bail

142   In some cases it may be possible for medical reports to be prepared before the hearing of a case begins, for production if required. Otherwise, they will be asked for during remand or following committal for trial, in which case the patient will be either in custody or on bail.

143   Under Section 3(6)(*d*) of the Bail Act 1976, a defendant granted bail may be required to comply with such requirements as appear to the court necessary to ensure that he makes himself available for the purpose of enabling enquiries or a report to be made to assist the court in dealing with him for the offence.

144   In some cases – for example, where the offender is known to be under the care of the District Health Authority – a court which requires medical reports may approach the District Medical Officer (in Wales the District Health Authority CAMO) to advise where the offender should be required to attend for examination as a condition of bail. In other cases, the court will wish to direct the offender to a hospital. For this purpose, Regional Health Authorities (in Wales District Health Authorities) are asked to send to each magistrates' court in their area a list of psychiatric clinics at which offenders may be required to attend as a condition of bail. Magistrates' courts are asked to give any doctor to whom an offender is so referred any information they have about any previous medical treatment. The doctor to whom the offender is first referred will be expected, after examining him, to decide what second doctor he ought to see, making the choice according to the circumstances of the case (eg general practitioners, doctor on the staff of the hospital to which admission might be desirable), and to make the necessary arrangements. One of the two doctors must be one who is approved under Section 12 of the Act. In cases where there is a considerable interval between the time when the person is committed for trial and the hearing of his case, it may be necessary to arrange for him to come to the clinic for further examination shortly before the date of the trial.

Arrangements for reports on defendants in custody

145   When the remand or committal for trial is in custody, the medical officer of the prison or remand centre will normally ask the Regional Health

Authority (in Wales the DHA) for the Region (Welsh District) in which the prison or centre is situated to arrange for a doctor, usually from the staff of the local hospital, to visit and examine the patient. If the medical officer of the prison or remand centre is not himself approved under Section 12 of the Act, the doctor called in to examine the patient must be one who is so approved.

Need for separate medical reports from each doctor

146   Each of the two doctors must make a separate report to the court – though one may, if he wishes, merely express agreement with the views and recommendations of the other. The immediate object of the reports is to give the court the medical evidence on which it may, if it thinks fit, found a hospital or guardianship order, or to inform the court that in the opinion of the reporting doctors the grounds for such an order do not exist. In order to comply with Section 37(4) the doctors will have to arrange for someone representing the managers of the relevant hospital to give written or oral evidence that a place will be available within 28 days. If they do not consider detention in hospital or guardianship necessary they should say so, and may indicate for the assistance of the court any other form of care or treatment which, if the court did not impose a sentence involving detention, they would consider useful – eg informal hospital treatment as an in-patient or out-patient, with or without a requirement in a probation order under Section 3 of the Powers of Criminal Courts Act 1973, or informal care from local social services. If the doctors recommend a hospital order they should indicate in their reports, in order to help the court to decide whether to make a restriction order, whether they consider the offender's mental condition to be such that, if he is at large, there is a risk of his committing offences of serious harm to the public. If admission to hospital, guardianship or informal community care is recommended, acceptance from a hospital or local social services authority must be sought – see para 153 below. The doctors' reports should be sent to the court before the date on which the offender is bailed to appear.

147   The Act requires two reports before a hospital order is made, but there is no limit to the number of doctors who may examine the patient (the defence may, for example, commission further reports) and there is nothing to prevent two reports being furnished to the court even if other doctors have disagreed on the need for hospital treatment. It is, however, desirable that the court should be aware of any difference of view.

47

Ascertaining the availability of a hospital bed

148   If the doctors wish to recommend admission to hospital, either on a hospital order, or probation order, or informally, one of them should first ascertain that a bed is actually available for that patient in a suitable hospital, or will be available within 28 days of the date on which the court will determine the case. The doctor responsible for seeking a vacancy is also responsible for ensuring that the court is informed whether a bed is available. He may either obtain a written statement from a doctor on the staff of the hospital and send it in with his report, or he may obtain the necessary undertaking informally and include it as part of his own report. In practice, this will often be a hospital at which the reporting doctor is himself on the staff. If admission to a special hospital is thought necessary, application should be made to the Department of Health and Social Security, not direct to the hospital (see paras 266–271).

Place of safety pending admission to hospital

149   If the hospital can admit the patient within 28 days of the court's sitting, but not immediately, the court may make a hospital order and also make an order under Section 37(4) for the patient to be detained in a place of safety while waiting admission to the hospital. 'Place of safety' is defined to include any hospital the managers of which are willing to receive the patient. In such a case, the doctor seeking a bed should, if possible, secure an undertaking from another hospital (eg a hospital with beds set aside for emergency cases) to accept the patient for the interim period. If there is difficulty in obtaining a bed, the doctor may need to seek the help of the Regional Health Authority (in Wales the District Health Authority).

Courts' power to request health authorities for information about hospital places

150   **Section 39** places a duty on Regional Health Authorities (in Wales the Secretary of State) to respond to requests from courts for information about a hospital or hospitals which could admit a person in respect of whom the court is considering making a hospital order. This implies the need to ensure that the facilities of the Region offer in total a comprehensive service for the Region's patients, both offenders and non-offenders. The court will not be obliged to go through the RHA if a placement can be arranged directly. If one of the doctors examining the patient is on the staff of the hospital to which admission might be desirable (see para 144) there should be no need

for such a request. There may sometimes be doubt as to the patient's normal place of residence or as to other factors which affect the appropriate hospital for admission, and in this case it will fall to the Regional Health Authority to advise the court.

151   A court with a request for information will contact the Regional Medical Officer for the Regional Health Authority covering the area from which the offender seems to come. In Wales this responsibility formally lies with the Secretary of State and the court should contact the Welsh Office in the first instance. However, in practice the responsibility will normally be delegated to a District Health Authority by the Secretary of State. (It should be noted that the Authority approached by the court is under a statutory duty to provide information about hospitals 'in its Region or elsewhere' at which arrangements could be made for persons to be admitted; so if the Authority first contacted believes it to be more appropriate for another Authority to respond, it will only be able to pass responsibility on if the second Authority and the court agree.) In order to fulfil this responsibility the Regional Health Authority (in Wales, the District Health Authority) should compile a summary of admission policies for the hospitals and units in each of its districts, so that the right placement for a particular patient can normally be readily ascertained; such a summary should assist the Authority to review the total pattern and develop plans as necessary to achieve a comprehensive service.

152   Where no hospital order is made, the court will dispose of the case under its normal penal powers. It may be willing to make an order of absolute or conditional discharge or impose a nominal penalty on the understanding that admission will be arranged as soon as possible under Part II of the Act or that the offender will receive out-patient treatment or be under informal supervision by the local authority during the interim period. The court may however in some cases consider it wiser to impose a sentence of detention with a view to the Home Secretary making a direction for the offender's transfer to hospital when a vacancy becomes available.

Community care – need to consult social service authorities

153   If the reporting doctors wish to recommend community care from the local social services authority with or without guardianship, they should consult the local social services authority for the patient's home area. It will be for the local social services authority to inform the court whether it is prepared to provide community care, including, if necessary, itself acting as guardian; if a private guardian is proposed it will be for the local social

services authority to inform the court that it has approved the proposed guardian and to send a statement signed by him that he is willing to act.

Detention in a place of safety

154   If an order is made for a patient's detention in hospital as a place of safety under Section 37(4) while awaiting admission to the hospital named in the hospital order, he may be detained there for not more than 28 days. There are no provisions for discharge or leave of absence. If the patient escapes, Section 138 allows him to be retaken by the person who had his custody immediately before his escape or by a constable or by any member of staff of, or person authorised in writing by the managers of, the hospital named in the hospital order. If the hospital order was not accompanied by a restriction order, he may not be retaken after the time limits described in Section 18(4). If the hospital order was accompanied by a restriction order, he may be retaken without limit of time. Section 50(4) provides in effect that time ceases to run while ex-prisoner patients (who represent the majority of patients subject to restrictions of fixed duration) are at large; or they remain liable to recapture indefinitely. If he is retaken, the time during which he was absent does not count towards the 28 days for which he may be detained in the place of safety.

155   Where it proves impossible to admit the patient to the hospital specified in the order within the 28 day period, the Secretary of State for Social Services (or the Secretary of State for Wales for hospitals in Wales) may give directions for the patient's admission to some other hospital; but in practice it is generally easier for the patient to be returned to court and for a further order to be made so as to give a further 28 days period in which a bed may become available.

Rights of appeal against conviction and sentence

156   All patients admitted to hospital on a hospital order will have certain rights of appeal either to the Court of Appeal (Criminal Division) or the Crown Court. A leaflet describing the rights of appeal and the appeal procedure is available for the hospitals concerned (leaflet 12), so that they can advise any patient who wishes to appeal of the procedure to be followed. If a patient appeals from the decision of a magistrates' court to the Crown Court he must be present in court when his appeal is heard. On the day of the hearing, of which the hospital authorities will be notified by the Crown Court, he should be taken to the court with an escort. If the patient appeals

to the Court of Appeal, he will not necessarily have to appear before the court, but if the court orders him to be present he should similarly be taken with an escort. If any patient who is required to appear before the court is, in the opinion of the responsible medical officer, unfit to appear, the Crown Court or the Registrar of Criminal Appeals, as the case may be, should be notified immediately. If on appeal the patient's conviction is quashed or another sentence is substituted for the hospital order the authority for his detention in hospital lapses automatically (but see para 133).

Effect of a hospital order without restrictions or of a guardianship order

157 The effect of a hospital order is, first, to confer authority on a constable, an approved social worker or any other person directed by the court to convey the patient to the hospital specified in the order within 28 days and, second, to confer authority on the managers of the hospital to admit the patient within that period and to detain him.

158 The effect of a guardianship order is to confer on the authority or person named in the order the same powers as a guardianship application made and accepted under Part II of the Act.

159 A patient admitted to hospital under a hospital order without restrictions or placed under guardianship by a guardianship order is treated essentially the same as a patient admitted to hospital or placed under guardianship under Part II of the Act. The necessary modifications to the provisions of Part II are made in Part I of Schedule 1 to the Act. A major difference between a Part III patient and one admitted under Part II is that the power of the patient's nearest relative to discharge him from hospital or guardianship under Section 23(2) does not apply to Part III patients. A further difference is that a patient admitted under a hospital order does not have the right to apply to a Mental Health Review Tribunal until six months after the date of the making of the order, if the order is renewed.

Effect of a hospital order with a restriction order

160 When a patient is admitted to hospital on a hospital order accompanied by a restriction order he is subject to the special restrictions and modifications set out in Sections 41 and 42 of the Act.

161 The patient may not be given leave of absence or be transferred to another hospital or to guardianship or be discharged except with the Home Secretary's consent, although a restricted patient can also apply to be

discharged by a Mental Health Review Tribunal – see para 218 below. Requests for consent to leave of absence, transfer or discharge should be sent to the Home Office by the responsible medical officer or the managers. When consent to transfer is given, the document in which consent is given should be attached to the authority for transfer and sent with it to the receiving hospital, a copy being kept by the hospital which the patient is leaving.

162 The authority for detention does not expire while the restriction order is in force. It does not, for instance, expire if a patient absents himself without leave and is not returned to hospital within the periods mentioned in Section 18; the patient may be returned to the hospital under that Section at any time so long as the restriction order is in force. Similarly, the six months limit on leave of absence, at the end of which the authority for detention expires under Section 17, does not apply. The provisions for expiry and renewal under Section 20 also do not apply; nor do the provisions for reclassification under Section 16.

163 It is, however, the duty of the responsible medical officer to keep continually under review the suitability for discharge of all patients who are subject to restriction on discharge, as of all other patients, and under Section 41(6) he is obliged to report at least annually to the Home Secretary on each restricted patient in his care. The initiative in seeking the Home Secretary's consent to discharge lies with the responsible medical officer and the managers, and they should not hesitate to seek consent when they consider the patient's condition warrants it. The Home Secretary may sometimes think it necessary, in view of his special responsibility for the protection of the public, to refuse or postpone his consent to discharge, but he will rely on the hospital authorities to bring cases to his notice. Hospital managers should not assume that consent to discharge will not be given before the end of the period named in a restriction order made for a limited time, since the Home Secretary has discretion to consent to discharge at any time.

164 In addition to his power to consent to discharge by the responsible medical officer or by the managers, the Home Secretary is given power under Section 42(2) to discharge patients subject to restriction orders himself. If the Home Secretary (or a Tribunal) discharges a patient the discharge may be conditional or absolute. A patient who is conditionally discharged may be recalled to hospital by the Home Secretary at any time during the currency of the restriction order. The conditions which the Home Secretary would normally think it appropriate to attach to a conditional discharge are that the patient should live in a particular household and be under the supervision of a psychiatrist and a responsible person (usually a probation

officer or social worker) who would undertake to submit reports to the Home Secretary on the patient's progress from time to time and to inform the Home Secretary and the responsible medical officer if the patient's mental condition appeared to be deteriorating.

165 If a patient subject to a restriction order is absent from the hospital without leave for more than 24 hours the Home Office should be informed, and also told when he returns. The local police should also be notified – see para 289 of this memorandum.

166 A restriction order ceases to have effect at the end of any period named in the order by the court or may be brought to an end at any time on the direction of the Home Secretary under Section 42(1). When this happens, Section 41(5) provides that the patient is to be treated as though he had been admitted to hospital in pursuance of a hospital order without a restriction order made on the date on which the restriction order ceased to have effect.

Notification of hospital orders to the Home Office

167 When a patient is admitted to hospital under a hospital order, the hospital is asked to send to the Home Office a copy of each order. This applies both to hospital orders made together with a restriction order and to those made without, but not to interim hospital orders, place of safety orders, remands to hospital or patients admitted by direction of the Home Secretary. However, if a patient originally admitted to hospital in one of the latter ways subsequently becomes subject to a hospital order, the hospital should notify the Home Office as if the patient were a new admission. The address to which copies of hospital orders should be sent is:
Home Office
Statistical Department
S2 Division
Room 844
Queen Anne's Gate
London
SW1H 9AT

Transfer to hospital of prisoners

168 Sections 47 to 53 make provisions for the transfer on the direction of the Home Secretary from penal institutions to hospitals of people suffering from mental disorder. Different considerations apply to sentenced prisoners

from those which apply to unsentenced prisoners because of the need ultimately to bring the latter before a court or to resolve in some other way the proceedings in which they are involved. There are further distinctions between different categories of unsentenced prisoners. Sections 47, 49 and 50 apply to sentenced prisoners: Sections 48, 49 and 51–53 apply to the various categories of unsentenced prisoners.

Sentenced prisoners

169   The power to transfer sentenced prisoners applies to any person serving a sentence of imprisonment or other form of detention.

170   The power may be exercised only if:
a.   the Home Secretary is satisfied, by reports from at least two registered medical practitioners, one of whom must be approved under Section 12:
   i.   that the prisoner is suffering from mental illness, psychopathic disorder, severe mental impairment or mental impairment; *and*
   ii.   that the mental disorder is of a nature or degree which makes it appropriate for the prisoner to be detained in a hospital for medical treatment; *and*
   iii.   in the case of a prisoner suffering from psychopathic disorder or mental impairment, that such treatment is likely to alleviate or prevent a deterioration of his condition; *and*
b.   both medical reports describe the prisoner as suffering from the same form or one of the same forms of disorder; *and*
c.   the Home Secretary is of the opinion, having regard to the public interest and all the circumstances, that it is expedient to direct the prisoner's transfer.

171   If transfer to a hospital (other than a special hospital) is recommended, the Regional Health Authority (in Wales the DHA) for the patient's home area will be sent copies of the medical reports and will be asked to say which hospital can admit the patient. In the case of a prisoner suffering from mental illness, this will be done by the prison medical officer at the same time as he sends the report to the Home Office; the RHA should notify both the Home Office and the prison which hospital will take the patient. In the case of prisoners suffering from other forms of mental disorder, the approach to the RHA will be made by the Home Office itself after preliminary consideration of the reports; the notification of the vacancy should be sent to the Home Office. On being informed that a vacancy is available, the Home Office will if satisfied that it is right to do so issue a transfer direction – ie a warrant directing the patient's transfer.

Sentenced prisoners – transfer directions with or without restriction directions

172 A transfer direction has the same effect as a hospital order made by a court without an order restricting discharge (see paras 157–159). (But it cannot specify a mental nursing home as the hospital to which the patient is to be admitted.) The direction is valid for 14 days, after which a fresh direction will be necessary if the patient has not been admitted to hospital.

173 When giving a transfer direction in respect of a sentenced prisoner, the Home Secretary has discretion also to give a restriction direction under Section 49. This direction has the same effect as a restriction order made by the court (see paras 160–166).

174 A restriction direction ceases to have effect on the date when the prisoner's sentence would have ended if he had remained in prison. Under Section 50(3) this date is calculated taking into account any remission of sentence to which the prisoner was entitled before transfer. Hospitals will be notified at the time of transfer of the date on which restrictions will expire. But if a patient has been absent without leave before that date the period of absence does not count towards the period of sentence. If any such patient is absent without leave for more than 24 hours, the hospital should inform the Home Office of the absence and when he returns to the hospital. The Home Office will then advise the hospital of the effect on the period of restriction.

175 Where both a transfer direction and a restriction direction are in force, the Home Secretary may direct the patient's return to prison (or other penal institution) or discharge him from the hospital on the same terms on which he could be released from prison. Before he can return a patient to prison the Home Secretary must first be notified by the responsible medical officer or any other registered medical practitioner or a Mental Health Review Tribunal that the patient no longer requires treatment in hospital for mental disorder or that no effective treatment for his disorder can be given in the hospital to which he has been transferred. The responsible medical officer should notify the Home Office at once in writing if he considers that a patient meets these criteria. If the Home Secretary decides that the patient should be returned to a prison or other institution he will issue a warrant directing the patient's removal from the hospital under section 50 of the Act.

176 The restriction on discharge on any patient transferred under Section 47 may be terminated at any time by the Home Secretary. When this is done, or when the period of restriction indicated in the transfer direction expires, the position of the patient and his nearest relative will be as described in para 159. The patient may also be discharged from hospital with the consent of

the Home Secretary and in certain circumstances by a Mental Health Review Tribunal (see para 227).

Other prisoners

177   The power to transfer prisoners other than those covered by Section 47 applies to
a.   all other persons detained in a prison or remand centre, including
b.   persons remanded in custody by a magistrates' court, and
c.   civil prisoners other than those covered by Section 47, and
d.   persons detained under the Immigration Act 1971.

178   The power may be exercised only if the Home Secretary is satisfied by reports similar to those required under Section 47 that:
a.   the prisoner is suffering from mental illness or severe mental impairment; *and*
b.   the mental illness or severe mental impairment is of a nature or degree which makes it appropriate for the prisoner to be detained in hospital for medical treatment; *and*
c.   the prisoner is in urgent need of such treatment.

179   As with transfer directions given under Section 47, both reports must describe the prisoner as suffering from the same form or at least one of the same forms of mental disorder, and the direction is valid for 14 days. The effect of the direction is the same (see para 172). When giving a transfer direction in respect of a prisoner in categories a. and b. of paragraph 177 the Home Secretary *must* also give a restriction direction, and when giving a transfer direction in respect of a prisoner in categories c. and d. he *may* give a restriction direction.

180   The consequences of a transfer direction given in respect of a prisoner in category a. of para 177 are as follows. (In such cases there will invariably be a restriction direction as well, as explained in the previous paragraph.) The transfer direction will cease to have effect when the patient's case has been fully dealt with by the appropriate court. Alternatively, if meanwhile the Home Secretary is notified by the responsible medical officer, any other registered medical practitioner or a Mental Health Review Tribunal that:
i.   the patient no longer requires treatment in hospital for mental disorder; or
ii.   no effective treatment for his disorder can be given in the hospital to which he has been transferred.
the Home Secretary *may* direct the patient's return to prison (or other penal institution).

181   Another alternative is that the court may order the patient to be returned to prison or released on bail if it is satisfied on the written or oral evidence of the responsible medical officer as to either of the conditions in i. or ii. above. Finally, if:

a.   it appears to the court that it is impracticable or inappropriate to bring the patient before it; and

b.   the court is satisfied, on the written or oral evidence of at least two registered medical practitioners, that the patient is suffering from mental illness or severe mental impairment of a nature or degree which makes it appropriate for the patient to be detained in a hospital for medical treatment,

the court may make a hospital order (with or without a restriction order) in the patient's absence and, in the case of a person awaiting trial, without convicting him.

182   The consequences of a transfer direction given in respect of a prisoner in category b. of para 177 are as follows. (In these cases too there will invariably be a restriction direction as explained in para 179.) The transfer direction will cease to have effect on the expiration of the period of remand to which the prisoner was subject unless he is then committed in custody to the Crown Court. The prisoner may be further remanded without being brought before the court, but only if he has appeared before the court in the previous six months; and if the prisoner is further remanded in custody the transfer direction will continue in effect. Alternatively, the magistrates' court may terminate the transfer direction if satisfied, on the written or oral evidence of the responsible medical officer, that the patient no longer requires treatment in hospital for mental disorder or that no effective treatment can be given in the hospital to which he has been transferred. The magistrates' court may conduct committal proceedings in the absence of the patient, if satisfied on the written or oral evidence of the responsible medical officer that the patient is unfit to take part in the proceedings and if the patient is legally represented; and if the patient is committed to the Crown Court and the magistrates' court has not terminated the transfer direction on the grounds that the patient no longer requires treatment, etc, the provisions of Section 51 (see para 180) will apply.

183   The consequences of a transfer direction given in respect of a prisoner in categories c. or d. of para 177 are as follows. In all cases the direction will cease to have effect on the expiry of the period during which the prisoner would have been liable to be detained. However, in cases where a restriction direction has been given as well as the transfer direction, the Home Secretary may direct the patient's return to prison if he is notified by the responsible medical officer, any other registered medical practitioner or a Mental

Health Review Tribunal, that the patient no longer requires treatment in hospital for mental disorder or that no effective treatment for his disorder can be given in the hospital to which he has been transferred.

Detention during Her Majesty's pleasure

184   Section 46 of the Act applies in the comparatively unusual circumstances where a serviceman is found to be not guilty by reason of insanity or unfit to stand trial by a court-martial and ordered to be detained 'during Her Majesty's pleasure', ie indefinitely. It gives the Home Secretary power to direct the detention of such a person in hospital (but not in a mental nursing home) as if subject to a hospital order with restrictions.

Criminal Procedure (Insanity) Act 1964

185   Under the Criminal Procedure (Insanity) Act 1964 a defendant before the Crown Court may be found either 'not guilty by reason of insanity' or 'under disability', ie 'unfit to plead'. In the event of either of these findings the court must make an order under Section 5(1) of that Act. The effect of this is that the defendant must be admitted within 2 months to 'such hospital as may be specified by the Secretary of State' (including a mental nursing home), where he will be detained as if he were subject to a hospital order together with a restriction order without limit of time.

186   Where such an order is made, therefore, the defendant will first be detained in a place of safety (as with a hospital order). The place of safety may be a hospital if the managers are willing temporarily to receive him. When a patient is admitted in this way a copy of the court order should be sent immediately to the Home Office. In sending the copy of the order to the Home Office, the hospital authorities should indicate whether they are willing to continue to detain the patient.

187   The Home Secretary will normally, on receiving notification of the order from the court, approach the relevant Regional Health Authority – in Wales the relevant District Health Authority – (or the DHSS where a place in a special hospital is considered appropriate), explaining the circumstances and asking for a suitable hospital place to be found. This will be a matter of considerable urgency, as the statutory period of two months cannot be extended. The Home Secretary is under an inescapable statutory obligation to specify a hospital, and in the last resort is bound to do so even if a hospital's agreement to admit the patient has not first been obtained. The specified hospital is under a legal obligation to admit the patient.

188 Because a patient admitted to hospital under the Criminal Procedure (Insanity) Act 1964 who has been found unfit to plead will not have been tried he may, if he recovers sufficiently, be remitted to prison by warrant of the Home Secretary for this purpose. The general principle observed is that a person who has been accused of an offence ought, if possible, to be brought to trial so that he may have an opportunity of having his guilt or innocence determined by a court. The Home Secretary will consult the responsible medical officer about such a patient's fitness for trial during the first six months of detention, at the end of which period the patient's case, if he has not already applied, will be referred automatically to a Mental Health Review Tribunal for their consideration (see para 220).

Part IV   Consent to treatment

Introduction

189   Part IV (Sections 56–64) is largely concerned with consent to treatment for mental disorder by long term detained patients in NHS hospitals and mental nursing homes, but certain safeguards in this part of the Act also apply to informal patients. There are two levels of safeguards. The first level applies to the most serious treatments which require a patient's informed consent *and* a second opinion (it is these safeguards which apply to informal patients). The second level applies to other serious treatments which require a patient's consent or a second opinion. All these safeguards can however be set aside where the need for treatment is urgent. The Act itself specifies two treatments to which the different levels of safeguards must be applied – ie psychosurgery which will require a patient's informed consent *and* a second opinion; and drug treatment for more than three months which will require the patient's consent *or* a second opinion. The Act provides for other treatments to be specified in regulations or in the Code of Practice (see paras 191, 195 and 253 below) which also gives guidance in relation to the medical treatment of mental disorder in general. Any treatment for mental disorder not specified in the Act, Regulations or Code of Practice may be given without the patient's consent by or under the direction of the rmo. Mental Health Act Commission guidance for responsible medical officers on the provisions of the Act governing consent to treatment and on the procedures to be followed when considering treatment are given in circular DDL(84)4. Further relevant information, including form MHAC/1, is contained in the MHAC letter dated September 1984.

Patients to whom Part IV applies

190   Section 56 provides that this part of the Act applies, with certain exceptions, to all detained patients, and extends to informal patients the provisions governing the most serious treatments requiring informed consent and a second opinion. The *exceptions* are:

a. patients detained by virtue of an emergency appication for assessment but for whom the second medical recommendation has not yet been given or received (Section 4);
b. in-patients detained for 72 hours on a report by their doctor (Section 5(2)) or for up to six hours under the nurse's holding power (Section 5(4)); accused persons remanded to hospital for a report on their mental condition (Section 35); offenders admitted to hospital as a place of safety under a direction made by the court for a period of up to 28 days following the making of a hospital order (Section 37(4)); persons suffering or believed to be suffering from mental disorder removed to a place of safety by a warrant made under Section 135 or found in a public place and removed to a place of safety under Section 136 for up to 72 hours.
c. a patient who has been conditionally discharged under Section 42(2), 73 or 74 and has not been recalled to hospital.

Patients in categories (a) to (c) above are in the same position as informal patients with regard to treatment (except that they are not covered by Section 57) and Common Law rules apply.

Treatment requiring consent *and* a second opinion

191   Only one treatment, psychosurgery, is specified in the Act as a treatment requiring consent and a second opinion (Section 57). Other treatments can be specified in Regulations or in the Code of Practice. (One treatment is specified in the Regulations – the surgical implantation of hormones for the purpose of reducing male sexual drive (Statutory Instrument 1983 No. 893, The Mental Health (Hospital, Guardianship and Consent to Treatment) Regulations 1983 (Regulation 16)).

Obtaining and validating consent

192   If it is thought desirable to treat a patient with psychosurgery or any other most serious treatment (or a series of treatments – see para 197 below), specified for this section, the rmo[1] should seek the consent of the patient in the normal way. If the patient is not considered to be capable of informed consent, or he does not consent, he cannot be given the treatment. If the patient consents to the treatment and appears to have understood the rmo's explanation of the nature, purposes and likely effects of the treatment, the rmo should contact the relevant office of the Mental Health Act

---

[1] In this part of the Act rmo means the registered medical practitioner in charge of the patient's treatment.

Commission (see para 255 et seq and Appendix 1). The Commission will send a medical practitioner appointed by them, who may be a medical member of the Commission, and two other appointed persons, who are not doctors (who will probably be non-medical members of the Commission), to consider the validity of the patient's consent. They must be allowed access to all the patient's records, including medical records and documents relating to his detention (if he is detained), and they must be allowed to interview, or in the case of the doctor examine, the patient in private if they wish (see Section 120, 121 and 129). Directions about giving access to persons authorised by the Mental Health Act Commission are contained in Circular HC(83)19.

Obtaining a second opinion

193   If the appointed medical practitioner, and the two other appointed persons, agree that the consent is valid they will jointly issue a certificate to the effect that the patient is capable of understanding the nature, purpose and likely effects of the treatment in question and has consented to it (form 37 Part 1). This certificate is not a substitute for a standard consent form which should be obtained. The appointed medical practitioner has also to consider whether the treatment is appropriate, and, if he is satisfied as to this, will issue a certificate to the effect that, having regard to the likelihood of the treatment alleviating or preventing a deterioration of the patient's condition, it should be given (form 37 Part II).

Need for second opinion giver to consult others professionally concerned

194   Before he issues this certificate the appointed medical practitioner has an obligation (under Section 57(3) of the Act) to consult a nurse, and one other person (not a nurse or doctor, probably a psychologist, social worker or other therapist), who have been professionally concerned with the patient's treatment. The rmo will need to provide the appointed medical practitioner with the relevant documents and the names of professionals involved with the case. Arrangements should then be made for the appointed medical practitioner to see the professionals he wishes to see. It is a requirement that any certificate issued under this part of the Act must be retained with the patient's records so that they can be inspected at any time by the Commission (see HC(83)19). These two certificates (which together make up form 37) constitute the authority for carrying out the treatment.

Treatment requiring consent *or* a second opinion

195   Section 58 applies to drug treatment if three months or more have elapsed since drugs were first given during that period of detention, and to any other form of treatment for detained patients that may be specified in Regulations. There can only be one three month period for drug treatment in any continuous period of detention, including such a period during which detention under one Section is immediately followed by detention under another Section. Unlike Section 57, there is no power for treatments for the purposes of Section 58 to be specified in the Code of Practice.

Regulation 16 specifies electroconvulsive therapy for the purposes of this Section. The effect of this Section on patients detained before 30 September 1983 is described in para 308.

Procedure for obtaining consent or a second opinion

196   If a patient consents to a treatment which comes under Section 58, and which the rmo has proposed and explained to the patient, the rmo (or a doctor appointed by the Commission) must certify in writing that the patient is capable of understanding the nature, purpose and likely effect of the treatment and has consented to it. He must use form 38 for this purpose whether or not he has also used a standard consent form. If the patient does not consent to a treatment included under this Section, and the rmo, having considered the alternatives, continues to feel that the patient needs that particular form of treatment, he should contact the relevant office of the Mental Health Act Commission. The Commission will send an appointed medical practitioner to consult with two persons professionally concerned with the patient, one of whom must be a nurse and the other neither a nurse nor a doctor, as well as the rmo, and give a second opinion as described above (para 194). The appointed medical practitioner, when certifying that having regard to the likelihood of the treatment alleviating or preventing a deterioration of the patient's condition, the treatment may be given, will also certify either that the patient is not capable of understanding the nature, purpose and likely effect of the treatment or that the patient has not consented to that treatment (form 39).

Plan of treatment

197   Section 59 states that any consent or certificate obtained for the purposes of Sections 57 or 58 can relate to a plan of treatment which can involve one or more of the treatments specified under the same Section and

can include a time scale for the administration of the treatments. If a plan of treatment is being considered, the appointed medical practitioner will consider the whole plan, and accept or reject it as a whole. However, it is hoped that there will be scope for discussion between the rmo and the appointed doctor about details of the plan, so that a generally sound plan need not be rejected because of a minor disagreement. An outline of the plan of treatment will appear on the certificate, and will, of course, be described in detail in the patient's medical records.

Withdrawing consent

198   Section 60 provides for a patient to withdraw his consent to any treatment which comes under Section 57 or 58. If a patient withdraws his consent from any treatment or plan of treatment under these Sections, the remainder of the treatment must be considered as a separate treatment for the purposes of those Sections. This means that if a patient withdraws his consent to a Section 57 treatment it must not be given, or if a plan of treatment is in progress, the treatment must cease immediately unless one of the criteria for urgent treatment described in para 202 below are met. If a patient withdraws consent to a treatment or a plan of treatment specified for Section 58 the rmo must contact the Mental Health Act Commission immediately so that the requirements of that Section can be complied with. Again, the rmo must cease administering the treatment unless Section 62 applies.

Reporting to the Commission

199   Section 61 provides that where the appointed persons have issued certificates under Section 57(2) or 58(3)(b) the rmo must give a report to the Commission on the treatment and the patient's condition:
a.   when he reviews the authority for detention under Section 20(3) (para 97);
b.   at any time the Commission requires him to do so.
Circular DDL(84)4 gives further information on Review of Treatment as does the MHAC letter dated September 1984.

200   In the case of a patient subject to a restriction order or direction the report must be made:
a.   six months after the date of the order or direction if the treatment was given in that period;

b.   if the treatment is given more than six months after the date of the order or direction, the next time the rmo makes a report under Section 41(6) or 49(7) (paras 163 and 173);

c.   at any time the Commission requires him to do so.

Commission's power to order that treatment be discontinued

201   Section 61 taken with Section 121(2) also provides that the Commission may at any time give notice to the rmo that a certificate given under Section 57(2) or 58(3)(b) no longer applies to treatment or plan of treatment after the date it specifies. After that date the rmo will again have to go through the procedures set out above (191–197) before he can continue treatment, unless the grounds for urgent treatment described in 202 et seq below are met.

Urgent treatment

202   Section 62 describes the circumstances under which Sections 57 and 58 do not apply, and in which treatments specified for those Sections may be given without the patient's consent, or to a patient who is not capable of giving informed consent. Any treatment may be given which is immediately necessary to save the patient's life. Treatments for mental disorder will, of course, rarely come into this category. Treatment of physical disorder is not covered by this Act, and doctors should follow their usual policy.

203   Other treatments which may be given are:

i.   a treatment which is not irreversible and is immediately necessary to prevent a serious deterioration of the patient's condition (a treatment is considered to be irreversible if it has unfavourable irreversible physical or psychological consequences);

ii.   a treatment which is not irreversible or hazardous and is immediately necessary to alleviate serious suffering by the patient (a treatment is considered to be hazardous if it entails significant physical hazard);

iii.   a treatment which is not irreversible or hazardous, is immediately necessary, and represents the minimum interference necessary, to prevent the patient from behaving violently or being a danger to himself or to others.

204   A course of treatment or a plan of treatment may be continued if the patient has withdrawn his consent, if the rmo considers that the discontinuance of the treatment or plan of treatment would cause serious suffering to the patient. In the case of Section 58 treatments the rmo will have to

contact the Mental Health Act Commission immediately for a second opinion, if one has not already been obtained (see 196 above). In all such cases treatment must cease as soon as its cessation will no longer cause *serious* suffering.

205   In cases where:
a.   the treatment is not immediately necessary; or
b.   it is proposed to continue treatment after the initial urgent administration;
the Mental Health Act Commission should be contacted. (Except in the case of Section 57 treatments where if the patient does not consent or cannot give informed consent, the treatment cannot in any case be given.)

Part V   Mental Health Review Tribunals

206   Each of the Regional Health Authorities in England is covered by a separate Mental Health Review Tribunal (MHRT). A separate Tribunal covers the whole of Wales. There are four Tribunal offices, three of which provide the administrative support to the Tribunals in England; the other provides administrative support for the Tribunal in Wales. Their addresses are set out at the end of this memorandum in Appendix 2. Further information is available from the Tribunal offices.

Patients detained under Part II of the Act
(this section does *not* apply to Part III patients. See paras 217–227 below)

Applications by patients or their nearest relatives

207   Patients in hospitals or under guardianship and their nearest relatives may apply to an MHRT on the occasions set out below:

	Patient may apply	*Nearest relative may apply*
Detained under Section 2	In first 14 days of detention	—
Detained under Section 3	In first 6 months of detention	—
Reclassified (Section 16)	In first 28 days from being informed of report by rmo	In first 28 days from being informed of report by rmo
Received into guardianship	In first 6 months of guardianship	—
Transferred to hospital from guardianship	In first 6 months of detention in hospital	—

	Patient may apply	Nearest relative may apply
Detention or guardianship is renewed	At any time in period for which detention is renewed	—
Rmo bars relative's discharge (Section 25)	—	In first 28 days from being informed of report by rmo
Nearest relative barred from acting as such by Order of County Court (Section 29)	—	In first 12 months of Order and subsequently once in each 12 month period for which Order is in force.

208   In each case only *one* application can be made in the period specified. This application can be made at any time during the period. An application which is withdrawn before it has been determined does not count for this purpose.

Hospital managers' duty to refer cases to a Tribunal

209   Any Part II patient who has been detained for 6 months under Section 3 or after being transferred from guardianship under Regulations made under Section 19 and who has not applied for a Tribunal or had an application made on his behalf by his nearest relative, or had his case referred by the Secretary of State, must be referred to a Tribunal by the hospital managers.

210   If the authority for detention is renewed, and the patient at that time has not had a Tribunal for three years or more, or, if he is under 16, for one year or more, the hospital managers must refer his case to a Tribunal.

Referral of cases by Secretary of State

211   The Secretary of State has the right to refer a patient to a Tribunal at any time.

Powers of the Tribunal

212   The Mental Health Review Tribunal have a range of options in relation to any patient whose case they consider. They have the power to

order discharge or delayed discharge from hospital or guardianship, or may recommend leave of absence or transfer to another hospital. If their recommendation is not complied with, they may reconvene.

213   The Tribunal *must* discharge a patient detained under Section 2 if they are satisfied that he is not then suffering from mental disorder 'of a nature or degree which warrants his detention in hospital for assessment (or for assessment followed by medical treatment) for at least a limited period', *or* if his detention is not justified in the interests of his health or safety or for the protection of others.

214   The Tribunal *must* discharge any other Part II patient if they are satisfied that he is not then suffering from one of the four categories of mental disorder (para 9 et seq) of a nature or degree which makes hospital treatment appropriate; *or* if his detention is not justified in the interests of his health or safety or for the protection of others, *or* – when the Tribunal is considering an application when the rmo has barred the patient's discharge by his nearest relative under Section 25 – if the patient, if released, would not be likely to act in a manner dangerous to others or to himself.

215   The Tribunal *may* discharge unrestricted patients in cases where the above criteria are not met (for restricted patients see below). In determining whether or not to do this, Section 72(2) directs that they should consider, except for Section 2 patients, the likelihood of medical treatment alleviating or preventing a deterioration of the patient's condition and, in the case of mentally ill or severely mentally impaired patients, the likelihood of the patient, if discharged, being able to care for himself, obtain the care he needs, or guard himself against serious exploitation.

216   The Tribunal *must* discharge a patient from guardianship if satisfied that he is not suffering from one of the four categories of mental disorder, *or* that it is not necessary in the interests of the welfare of the patient or for the protection of others that he should remain under guardianship.

Patients detained under Part III of the Act

Applications in first 6 months of detention

217   Different considerations apply to Part III patients. Such patients have the right to apply to the Tribunal in the first six months of detention only if they fall into one of the following categories:

a.   patients placed under guardianship order;
b.   patients originally detained subject to a restriction order, who remain in hospital after its expiry as if subject to a hospital order made on the date the restriction order expired;

c. patients originally detained under the Mental Health (Northern Ireland) Order 1986 and transferred to a hospital in England or Wales under Section 82;

d. patients originally detained under mental health legislation in the Channel Islands or the Isle of Man and transferred to a hospital in England or Wales under that legislation;

e. patients originally detained under the Mental Health (Scotland) Act 1984 and transferred to a hospital in England or Wales under Section 77 of that Act;

f. patients admitted to hospital under an order made under Section 5(1) of the Criminal Procedure (Insanity) Act 1964;

g. patients admitted to hospital under Sections 46, 47 or 48.

In the case of patients in categories a.–f., the six months begins from the date of the order or transfer direction: in the case of patients in category g., from the date of the transfer direction.

Hospital orders

218   Part III patients detained in hospital under a *hospital order* (with or without restrictions) have no right to apply in the first 6 months, because their case will have been examined at the outset by a court which must have considered medical evidence from two registered medical practitioners. These patients' first opportunity to apply to the Tribunal therefore arises in the second six months of detention (if detention is renewed in the case of unrestricted patients), and thereafter at annual intervals. These entitlements correspond to the rights accruing on renewal of the authority for detention of Part II patients.

219   The nearest relative of a patient detained in hospital (other than a restricted patient) also has the right to apply to the Tribunal at these intervals. The nearest relative of a patient placed under guardianship may apply at any time within the first 12 months and annually thereafter.

Referral of case by the Home Secretary or hospital managers

220   If a Part III patient has not had a Tribunal for three years, his case must be referred to a Tribunal, by the Home Secretary in the case of restricted patients, and the Hospital Managers in the case of other Part III patients. In addition, restricted patients admitted to hospital under Section 5(1) of the Criminal Procedure (Insanity) Act 1964 who do not exercise their right to apply to the Tribunal during the first six months of detention (see

para 188), or who withdraw any such application, must have their case referred to the Tribunal by the Home Secretary at the end of that period.

Conditionally discharged patients

221 Conditionally discharged restricted patients may also apply to the Tribunal 12 months after discharge and every 2 years thereafter, and if such a patient is recalled to hospital the Home Secretary must refer his case to the Tribunal within one month of his being readmitted to hospital.

Powers of the Tribunal in respect of restricted patients

222 The Tribunal's powers in respect of *non-restricted* Part III patients are the same as for Part II patients (see para 215), but they are different for restricted patients. Under Section 73 of the 1983 Act a Tribunal *must* order the *absolute discharge* of a patient subject to a restriction order if they are satisfied:

i. that he is not suffering from mental illness, psychopathic disorder, severe mental impairment or mental impairment or from any of those forms of disorder of a nature or degree which makes it appropriate for him to be liable to be detained in hospital for medical treatment;
    or
ii. that it is not necessary for the health or safety of the patient or for the protection of other persons that he should receive such treatment;
    and
iii. that it is not appropriate for the patient to remain liable to be recalled to hospital for further treatment.

223 Under the same Section the Tribunal *must* order the *conditional discharge* of a patient subject to a restriction order if it is satisfied that the patient should remain liable to recall, but:

i. that he is not suffering from mental illness, psychopathic disorder, severe mental impairment or mental impairment or from any of those forms of disorder of a nature or degree which makes it appropriate for him to be liable to be detained in a hospital for medical treatment;
    or
ii. that it is not necessary for the health or safety of the patient or the protection of other persons that he should receive such treatment.

224 Where a Tribunal decides to order the conditional discharge of a patient it may defer its final direction until the arrangements necessary for that purpose have been made. In practice, this means that the Tribunal will

require the detaining hospital to submit proposals for the patient's aftercare for the Tribunal's approval.

225 In the case of non-restricted patients, Tribunals 'shall have regard to' the likelihood of medical treatment alleviating or preventing a deterioration of the patient's condition. There is no equivalent of this provision in relation to restricted patients. The effect of this is that although the Tribunal must discharge if the mental disorder is not of a nature or degree which makes medical treatment appropriate (see para 7(g) for definition of medical treatment) the patient's susceptibility to the treatment being provided in that hospital forms no part of the statutory criteria which a Tribunal will have to consider before authorising the discharge of a restricted patient. The fact that a restricted patient's condition is not benefiting from the treatment he is receiving does not automatically entitle him to be discharged.

226 In the case of restricted patients the Tribunal has no discretion to discharge the patient if the statutory criteria for discharge set out in paragraphs 222 and 223 are not fulfilled.

Special provisions in respect of patients subject to a restriction direction

227 Patients subject to a restriction direction given by the Home Secretary (see para 172 et seq) are liable to resume serving their sentence of imprisonment or to be brought before a court to stand trial if they no longer require treatment in hospital. Under these circumstances, the Tribunal cannot therefore authorise discharge in the normal way. Instead, it has to notify the Home Secretary if it finds that the patient could otherwise be conditionally or absolutely discharged, and may at the same time recommend that if the patient cannot be conditionally discharged he should continue to be detained in hospital rather than being returned to prison. In the case of a patient who was originally a remand prisoner or other prisoner transferred under section 48, the Home Secretary has no discretion: unless the Tribunal has made a recommendation for the patient's retention in hospital, he must return the patient to prison. In the case of a *sentenced* prisoner, however, it may be that the Home Secretary is able to agree to his discharge. The Home Secretary has 90 days from the date of notification of the Tribunal's finding in which to give notice that the patient may be discharged: if he does not, the patient must be returned to prison unless the Tribunal has made a recommendation that in those circumstances he should remain in hospital.

General powers and procedures of Tribunals

228 In any non-restricted case before it, the Tribunal has power to reclassify the patient as suffering from a different form of mental disorder.

Conversely, even if the application was made under Section 16 when the patient is reclassified, the Tribunal may direct discharge or one of the other specified options.

Tribunal Rules

229   The Lord Chancellor has made Rules of Procedure under Section 78 – the Mental Health Review Tribunal Rules 1983 (Statutory Instrument 1983 No 942). These impose various duties on the 'responsible authority' – in the case of a patient detained in hospital, the managers and in the case of a patient detained under guardianship, the local social services authority.

Form of application

230   Although it is not essential for an application to be made on a pre-scribed form, a suitable form can be supplied to the applicant on request by either the Tribunal or the responsible authority. Hospitals in which patients are detained, and local social services authorities in whose area there are patients under guardianship, should therefore hold stocks of these forms – which can be obtained from the stationery office or, if only a small number is required, from the Clerk to the Tribunal. Staff should give patients and their relatives any help required to fill in the form. It would also be helpful if they would insert the name of the Regional Health Authority in the space provided before passing on the form to the patient or relative.

231   The Tribunal will send the responsible authority a copy of the application, and ask them to submit a statement giving certain information including a medical report by the responsible medical officer (the form of this Statement is set out in the Schedule to the Tribunal Rules). The authority should inform the Tribunal at once if the patient has no right to apply – eg if he is not subject to detention under the Act and is free to discharge himself. In all other cases they should forward their statement as soon as possible, and in any case within three weeks, and the Tribunal will then arrange a hearing in accordance with the Rules. Where the applicant is a restricted patient detained in hospital the Home Secretary will also provide a statement. Where the applicant is a conditionally discharged patient, the Home Secretary will provide the whole statement. The responsible authority or Home Secretary may ask, giving supporting reasons, that part of the statement be withheld from the patient (see Rules 6(4) and 12).

232   The Tribunal have the power under the Rules to obtain any information they think necessary, including the power to subpoena witnesses.

The medical member of the Tribunal will in all cases be required to examine the patient or take such other steps as he considers necessary to form an opinion on the patient's mental condition. In addition, any doctor authorised by the patient or applicant to the Tribunal may examine the patient in private and require any records relating to the patient's detention or treatment in hospital to be produced for his inspection.

Legal Aid and Assistance

233 Legal assistance under the Green Form Scheme is available to help patients and other applicants with limited means to prepare their cases. This assistance covers all the work done by a lawyer in preparing the case, including paying for an independent medical report where this is considered necessary by the lawyer. Patients may also be provided with legal representation at the hearing under the Assistance By Way of Representation (ABWOR) scheme. Before assistance of any kind may be given under the Green Form Scheme, the patient must undergo a simple assessment of resources carried out by his solicitor to ensure that he qualifies on financial grounds. In addition, when ABWOR is sought, the Law Society's approval must be obtained. Green forms are obtainable from the Law Society or Legal Aid Area Offices and will be held by any solicitor undertaking legal aid work. In addition both hospital managers and any member of staff, including a social worker, may obtain advice from the Area Offices to assist those detained patients who have no access to solicitors or legal advice. A list of Legal Aid Area Offices in England and Wales and the areas covered by them is at Appendix 3.

234 The responsible authority may be represented by anyone they authorise for this purpose. This will normally be the responsible medical officer who should be ready to answer any questions the Tribunal may have about the patient's suitability for discharge and his home circumstances. Other people, in particular social workers, may be brought in as witnesses when necessary. Legal representation is not usually necessary for the responsible authority.

235 Tribunals usually meet to deal with applications at the hospital in which the patient is detained. Hospitals are asked to make suitable rooms available for the Tribunal and anyone attending as a witness. A guide for the information of hospitals is available from the Tribunal offices.

Part VI   Removal and return of Patients within the United Kingdom

236   Part VI of the Act provides powers under which certain categories of detained patients and patients under guardianship may be moved between England and Wales and other parts of the United Kingdom, the Channel Islands and the Isle of Man, while remaining under detention or guardianship; or may be retaken in those places when absent without leave from hospitals or institutions. It also provides powers for moving mentally ill patients who are neither British citizens nor Commonwealth citizens with the right of abode here from hospitals in England and Wales to countries abroad. Appendix 5 to this memorandum gives a brief resumé of the procedures to be followed and the corresponding provisions in the Scotland and Northern Ireland mental health legislation.

Removal between England and Wales, Scotland, Northern Ireland, the Channel Islands and the Isle of Man

237   If arrangements are made at the request of a patient or his relatives for him to go to another part of the United Kingdom, the Channel Islands or the Isle of Man, and if it is not necessary to keep the authority for detention in operation while he is being moved, he may be discharged before leaving, and enter hospital or guardianship on the other side of the border under the admission procedures of that country, either compulsory or voluntary. On the other hand, if it is necessary to have powers of control over the patient while on the journey and immediately on arrival in the other country, the procedures described in Sections 80 to 85 may be used. These Sections define the categories of patients who may be moved without a break in the powers of detention or guardianship and how they are to be treated as regards powers of detention, guardianship, and discharge after arriving in the receiving country.

Removal from England and Wales

238   The suggestion that a patient should be moved from a hospital in England and Wales may originate from the patient himself or his relatives or

friends or from the hospital or other authority in whose care he is. Preliminary enquiries about arrangements for his care in the other country should be made before an approach is made to the Secretary of State whose authority for the removal is required under the relevant Section of the Act. The views of the person exercising the functions of the nearest relative should be ascertained and reported to the Secretary of State whenever it is desired to remove a patient under Section 80 or 81.

Removal to England and Wales

239   When a patient who is detained under the equivalent of Part II of the Act is moved to England or Wales under Section 82 or Section 77 of the Mental Health (Scotland) Act 1984 or under a corresponding provision of Channel Island or Isle of Man legislation, he is to be treated on arrival as though admitted to hospital on an application made under Sections 2 or 3 of the Act, or as though received into guardianship under Sections 7 and 8. He will have a right of application to a Mental Health Review Tribunal under Section 66(1) within 6 months of his transfer. The written authority for removal given by the appropriate authority at the patient's place of origin will be sent to the receiving hospital or guardian, and to the local social services authority if it is not the guardian and should be kept as the document authorising the patient's detention or guardianship in England and Wales. With it should be kept the record of the date of arrival at the hospital or other place where he is to reside, which is required by Regulation 11. The managers of the hospital should, if reasonably practicable, inform the patient's nearest relative, if any, of the admission.

240   The authority for detention or guardianship will expire if not renewed at the end of 6 months from that date, under Section 20 and all the other relevant provisions of Part II of the Act also apply. Section 92(3) and Regulation 11 require the responsible medical officer (or nominated medical attendant) to record the form of mental disorder from which the patient is suffering, in accordance with the classifications recognised under the Act in England and Wales, on form 32 as soon as possible after his arrival. In cases of reception into the guardianship of a person other than a local social services authority, the date of arrival is to be notified by the guardian to the responsible local social services authority, as well as the other notifications required under Regulation 12. He must also inform the nearest relative, if any, as soon as reasonably practicable, of the patient's reception into guardianship.

241   When a patient who is moved to England and Wales under the provisions described in the previous paragraph was before removal treated

as subject to a hospital order with or without a restriction order, he is to be treated on arrival as though admitted under the equivalent provision of Part III of the Act. Under Section 69(2)(*a*) *such a patient has a right of application to the Mental Health Review Tribunal* within the first 6 months, unlike most other Part III patients. Regulation 11 requires the responsible medical officer to record the patient's mental classification on his arrival (if he is not subject to restriction on discharge) or (if he is so subject) when the restriction ceases to have effect.

Removal of mentally ill aliens

242   Section 86 of the Mental Health Act empowers the Home Secretary to authorise the removal to any country abroad of a person who is neither a British citizen nor a Commonwealth citizen with the right of abode in the United Kingdom, who is receiving in-patient treatment for mental illness in England and Wales or Northern Ireland and who is detained pursuant to an application for admission for treatment, a hospital order or an order or direction having the same effect as a hospital order. The Home Secretary must be satisfied that proper arrangements have been made for the patient's care or treatment in the country to which he is to be moved, and *the proposal must have the approval of a Mental Health Review Tribunal*. In such cases the Home Secretary will exercise his discretionary power to refer the patient to a Tribunal. The Tribunal will be asked for advice whether removal would be in the best interests of the patient and whether proper arrangements have been made for his care or treatment.

243   Proposals for the removal of such a person from a hospital or mental nursing home should be made in the first place to the Home Office (C3 Division, Queen Anne's Gate, London SW1H 9AT). Details should be given of any arrangements which have been or could be made for the patient's care and treatment in the receiving country. The Home Office will, in consultation with the Department of Health and Social Security, decide whether authority under Section 86 should be issued or whether the patient should be repatriated under other powers. Application to the Home Office will not be necessary if the patient, whether or not accompanied by an escort, is able and willing to travel without powers of detention, and suitable arrangements have been made.

244   The types of cases in which it might be appropriate to propose repatriation include:
a.   those where repatriation would be in the person's interest;

b. those where the person has been in hospital in this country for a considerable period (6 months or more), where there is little prospect of a substantial improvement in his condition and where repatriation would not be deterimental to him.

245 Normally when a patient is removed from England and Wales under Section 86 the authority for his detention ceases to have effect forthwith. But where the patient is subject to a hospital order together with a restriction order, they will remain in force so that they will apply to the patient if he should return before they would otherwise have expired.

Retaking of patients

246 Sections 87 and 89 permit patients who are absent without leave from mental hospitals or institutions in Northern Ireland, the Channel Islands or the Isle of Man to be retaken if found in England and Wales. Equivalent provision in respect of patients from Scotland is made by Section 84 of the Mental Health (Scotland) Act 1984. The persons authorised to retake such patients are approved social workers or constables in England and Wales, who may be asked to co-operate with the Scottish, Northern Ireland, or Island authorities in such cases. Section 88 permits patients from England and Wales to be retaken in Scotland, Northern Ireland, the Channel Islands or the Isle of Man as mentioned in para 79 of this memorandum. All these provisions are subject to any time limits which apply to the retaking of patients in the country from which the patient is absent.

247 None of these Sections apply to patients under guardianship. The powers of guardians are in abeyance while a patient is not in the part of the United Kingdom in which the guardianship is in force. They revive if the patient returns while the authority for guardianship is still in force, ie if it has not lapsed under Section 18, 20, or 22, or been discharged under Section 23.

Part VIII   Miscellaneous functions of local authorities and the Secretary of State

Approved social workers

248   See Department of Health and Social Security circular LAC (86) 15.

249   Section 114(1) requires a local social services authority to appoint a sufficient number of approved social workers to carry out the functions given to them by the Act. Section 114(2) provides that nobody can be appointed as an approved social worker unless the local social services authority has approved him as having appropriate competence in dealing with people who are suffering from mental disorder. In appointing people as approved social workers, the local social services authority must follow the directions issued by the Secretary of State in circular LAC (86) 15 (Welsh Office Circular 51/86) (Section 114(3)).

Visiting patients

250   Local authorities continue to have a duty to arrange visits to certain patients in hospital or nursing homes whether or not the patients concerned are being treated for mental disorder (Section 116). Local authorities must also take such other steps in relation to these patients while they are in a hospital or nursing home as would be expected to be taken by the patient's parents. This Section applies to:

a.   a child or young person in respect of whom the rights and powers of a parent are vested in a local authority by virtue of Section 3 or 10 of the Child Care Act 1980, or Section 17 of the Social Work (Scotland) Act 1968.

b.   a person who is subject to the guardianship of a local social services authority under the 1983 Act (para 43 et seq) or the Mental Health (Scotland) Act 1984.

c.   a person the functions of whose nearest relative under the 1983 Act or the Mental Health (Scotland) Act 1984 are for the time being transferred to a local social services authority (para 109 et seq).

Aftercare

251 Section 117 reinforces the duty which already exists under other legislation for health and social services authorities (in co-operation with relevant voluntary agencies) to provide after care. It pinpoints three specific groups of detained patients whose discharge from hospital is to be followed by aftercare for as long as it is needed:
a. persons who have been detained under Section 3;
b. persons who have been admitted to hospital in pursuance of a hospital order under Section 37;
c. persons who have been admitted to hospital in pursuance of a transfer direction under Section 47 or 48.

Code of Practice

252 Section 118 requires the Secretary of State to prepare, publish and from time to time revise, a Code of Practice. The Code must include:
a. guidance in relation to compulsory admissions to hospitals and mental nursing homes under the Act;
b. guidance in relation to the medical treatment of patients suffering from mental disorder.
The Secretary of State directed the Mental Health Act Commission (para 255 et seq) to submit proposals as to the content of the Code, and the Commission is also responsible for submitting proposals for revisions to the Code. In particular they may want to propose revisions to it when developments in professional practice, or particular issues where guidance is needed, have come to their attention. It will be noted that b. is not confined to the treatment of detained patients. The Code does not have the force of law, but everyone involved in the care of mentally disordered patients, including treatment in the community, should have regard to it whenever it is relevant. Failure to do so could be evidence of bad practice.

253 Section 118(2) provides that the Code of Practice shall specify forms of medical treatment which give rise to special concern and should therefore only be given with consent and a second opinion (para 191 et seq). The forms of treatment specified in the Code will be in addition to any specified in the Regulations made under Section 57(1) (Regulation 16), and the forms of treatment so specified should be treated as Section 57 treatments.

254 During the preparation of the Code of Practice the Secretary of State consulted bodies which seemed to him to be concerned; he will do likewise should any revision of the Code be proposed. The Code is subject to the approval of Parliament and will be published.

The Mental Health Act Commission

255   The Mental Health Act Commission has been set up as a special health authority by the Secretary of State, and like other health authorities it has to comply with directions from him, but otherwise it is independent in the performance of its functions, and the advice it offers. Section 121(2) requires that the Secretary of State must direct the Commission to carry out certain functions listed there (see below). The Commission has been designated by an Order in Council under Section 109(d) of the NHS Act 1977 as an authority subject to the Health Service Commissioner's jurisdiction.

256   The Secretary of State for Social Services acting jointly with the Secretary of State for Wales is responsible for making appointments to the Commission. The membership of the Commission includes lawyers, nurses, psychologists, social workers and laymen in roughly equal numbers, with a larger number of doctors. Medical members of the Commission have more duties, for example, with regard to consent to treatment (para 192 et seq). The members of the Commission together have a wide range of experience and knowledge of the issues involved in the compulsory admission and medical treatment of mental patients. The members are divided into committees or panels based on three centres (see Appendix 1).

257   The Commission also has a central policy committee which takes the lead in preparing proposals for the Code of Practice and drafting the two yearly report on the Commission's activities.

258   The functions which the Secretary of State has directed the Commission to perform on his behalf are:
a.   appointing medical practitioners for the purposes of the Consent to Treatment provisions (paras 192 and 196). These appointed doctors may include Commissioners but there may be an additional number of psychiatrists who are not on the Commission;
b.   carrying out the function described in Section 61 (the review of treatment given only after a second opinion has been obtained) (para 199);
c.   carrying out the functions described in Section 120 (the visiting of patients and investigation of complaints) (para 262 et seq);
d.   submitting proposals for the Code of Practice (paras 252–254).
The Commission is also required by the Act to:
a.   produce a report every two years;
b.   review the decision to withhold a postal packet if an application is made to it to do so (Section 121(7)).

259   The Commission can also be directed by the Secretary of State, after

consultation, to look at any matter relating to the care and treatment of patients not detained under the Act (Section 121(4)). The Code of Practice (see above) does in any case cover treatment for mental disorder in general.

260 The Commission's functions are quite separate from those of Mental Health Review Tribunals (para 206 et seq) which determine whether a patient should continue to be detained. The Commission has no power to discharge a patient.

261 The Orders and Regulations concerning the functions, establishment, and constitution of the Commission are the Mental Health Act Commission Regulations 1983 (Statutory Instrument 1983 No 894), the Mental Health Act Commission (Establishment and Constitution) Order 1983 (Statutory Instrument 1983 No 892), The Health Service Commissioner for England (Mental Health Act Commission) Order 1983 (Statutory Instrument 1983 No 1114) and The Mental Health (Amendment) Act 1982 (Commencement No 1) Order 1983 (Statutory Instrument 1983 No 890 (c 24)).

The general protection of detained patients

262 Section 120 confers certain duties on the Secretary of State in connection with the general protection of detained patients. Section 121 provides that those duties are to be carried out by the Mental Health Act Commission. Accordingly Section 120(1) requires the Commission to keep under review the exercise of the powers conferred by the Act in relation to the detention of patients. The Commission is also required to make arrangements for persons authorised by it to visit and interview in private patients detained in hospitals and mental nursing homes. The authorised persons must also investigate any complaint which a detained patient thinks has not been dealt with satisfactorily by the hospital managers or any other complaint concerning the use of powers given by the Act. The Commission can investigate a complaint made by an ex-patient which he does not feel has been satisfactorily dealt with by the managers as long as it relates to a period of detention under the Act or any complaint made by a relative or friend of a patient, or by another person, in relation to that patient or ex-patient. Where such a complaint is made by a Member of Parliament the Commission are required to inform him of the results of any investigation carried out.

263 The Commission will direct any problems the detained patients have to the hospital managers or to other appropriate channels, but is also able to take up any matters where patients feel their grievance has not been resolved satisfactorily. The Commission does not replace or duplicate the

work of other individuals and bodies who are able to help patients with their problems, for example hospital managers, Community Health Councils, voluntary organisations, Members of Parliament and the Health Service Commissioner. The person/persons carrying out an investigation on behalf of the Commission can discontinue it if he/they thought it right to do so (for example because it was more suitable for investigation by the Health Service Commissioner), but will try to ensure that detained patients are helped with particular problems by the most appropriate person or body (Section 120(2)).

264   Any person authorised by the Commission has the right of access to detained patients and their records at any reasonable time. In the case of mental nursing homes this is achieved by virtue of Section 120(4). In the case of NHS hospitals this is achieved by the direction issued by the Secretary of State, notified in circular HC (83) 19, who also ensures that this happens in Special Hospitals. Authorised persons may visit, interview, and in the case of medical practitioners examine, in private, any detained patient. They may also require the production of and inspect any records relating to the detention or treatment of a detained mental patient (including admission documents, medical notes, records of seclusion etc).

265   As well as looking at individual patient's complaints, and seeing that proper authority exists for a patient's detention, the Commission also reviews the way in which the powers of detention are being exercised and monitors the working of the consent to treatment provisions. Members of the Commission will visit regularly every hospital or mental nursing home where a patient is detained, with more frequent visits to Special Hospitals. Commissioners may often be able and indeed will want to give notice of their intention to visit a hospital or mental nursing home, but they do not have to, and on occasions may prefer to visit unannounced. It is an offence under Section 129 to refuse an authorised person access to patient or records, or in any way obstruct him in carrying out his functions.

Special Hospitals

266   Special Hospitals are required to be provided by the Secretary of State for Social Services under Section 4 of the National Health Service Act 1977. There are four special hospitals: Broadmoor, Rampton, Moss Side and Park Lane. They provide the same range of therapeutic services as ordinary psychiatric hospitals but they are intended by virtue of the National Health Service Act 1977 for the treatment of patients who are detainable under the Mental Health Act and who, in the opinion of the Secretary of State, require

this treatment under special security because of their dangerous, violent or criminal propensities. The régimes of care and observation are such that they can only be justified when the highest level of security is required and no lesser degree of security would provide a reasonable safeguard to the public.

267   All admissions to special hospitals are determined centrally by the Department of Health and Social Security; formal applications should be made to the DHSS (PC4A), Alexander Fleming House, Elephant and Castle, London SE1 6BY. The Department will usually then arrange for a special hospital consultant to examine and report on the patient where this has not been done in advance. The final decision in all cases rests with the Department, acting on behalf of the Secretary of State, and the applicant will be advised of the outcome.

268   The application should contain a full account of the patient's psychiatric and social history, together with details of any criminal history and a full description of the circumstances which give rise to the application. It is not sufficient merely to list the charges and/or previous convictions or to summarise behaviour as 'aggressive', 'assaultive', 'dangerous' etc, without evidence of the nature of the dangerous behaviour and the circumstances in which it was used. Any references to absconding behaviour should give details of any incidents and pay particular attention to the amount of planning and determination involved. Supporting documents, such as depositions, can also be helpful. The application should also give reasons why treatment in secure conditions which fall short of the level of security in a special hospital is considered inappropriate.

269   Special hospital admission is *not generally* considered suitable for patients who:
i.   are suffering from severe mental impairment – unless there is a *strong probability* that the patient will seriously harm staff/other patients, if the opportunity presents;
ii.   though exhibiting extreme disruptive or anti-social behaviour in the community or local hospital are unlikely to inflict serious physical injury;
iii.   require close observation mainly to prevent self injury – unless this is associated with a *probability* of violence to others;
iv.   require asylum/long term care but for whom lesser conditions of security would provide adequate protection for the public;
v.   would simply benefit from the stability and support of a physically secure régime – unless they also present a risk of serious harm to the public at large;

vi. are under 16 years of age or over 60.

Provision of comprehensive facilities for such patients is the responsibility of regional and district health authorities. Any lack of local provision for difficult to place patients will not usually be accepted as a reason for admission to a special hospital.

270   Where the Department declines to make a special hospital bed available, the referring doctor and, where appropriate, defence solicitors and the courts will be notified of the reasons. It will be for the applicant to take up with the health authority concerned what suitable arrangements can be made to meet the needs of the patient concerned.

271   The conditions for admission described above will apply equally to patients liable to detention under civil powers, or hospital orders, or interim hospital orders, or remands to hospital for report/treatment and to those transferred from prison by direction of the Home Secretary.

Part X   Miscellaneous and supplementary provisions

Informal and emergency admissions

272   Informal admission should be the normal mode of admission to hospital, and should be used whenever a patient is not unwilling to be admitted, and can be treated without the use of compulsory powers (see Section 131). If compulsory detention becomes necessary in the case of an informal patient an application can be made under Section 5 (para 30). No hospital should have a rule specifying times of day when only formal patients will be admitted.

273   The attention of Regional Health Authorities (in Wales, District Health Authorities) is drawn to the fact that Section 140 places a statutory duty on them to notify local social services authorities of hospitals in the Region which have arrangements for admitting emergencies. This duty will be met if the Authority makes arrangements for social services authorities to be kept aware of psychiatric catchment areas for particular hospitals within the Region, with suitable notes explaining, for example, where the catchment area for elderly patients differs from that for younger patients. (RHAs must also provide the courts with information about hospital places if requested. See para 150 et seq.)

The duty of hospital managers to provide information

274   Sections 132 and 133 place a duty upon hospital managers to provide certain information to detained patients and their nearest relatives. Section 132(1) places a duty on hospital and mental nursing home managers to take such steps as are practicable to ensure that a detained patient understands:
a.   which Section of the Act for the time being authorises his detention and the effects of that Section;
b.   his right to apply to a Mental Health Review Tribunal (if applicable). This information must be given as soon as practicable after the commencement of the patient's detention and as soon as practicable after a different

Section of the Act is used to authorise his detention. In practice this will mean that the patient will have to be told immediately if he is detained for 72 hours or less. When the rmo, nurse or other professional gives this information to the patient he should be as helpful as possible, and try to explain to the patient any points he does not appear to understand. He should also hand the patient the written statement required by Section 132(1) and (3) (see para 276). Some patients will not be able to comprehend what they are told but the law requires an attempt to be made, and in the case of the short-term powers there may be little time to wait and see if a patient's powers of understanding improve.

275   Section 132(2) places a further duty on hospital managers to take such steps as are practicable to ensure that a detained patient understands the effect, so far as it is relevant to him, of the following Sections of the Act:

a.   Sections 23, 25 and 66(1)(g) which deal with the power of the rmo, the hospital managers and the nearest relative to discharge him (para 104 et seq);

b.   Part IV of the Act which deals with consent to treatment (para 189 et seq);

c.   Section 118 which deals with the Code of Practice (para 252 et seq);

d.   Section 120 which deals with the general protection of patients (para 262 et seq);

e.   Section 134 which deals with patients' correspondence (para 279 et seq);

In particular the intention is that the patient should understand the means by which his detention can be ended and the various safeguards from which he benefits including those concerning consent to treatment. The patient should also be told about any legal aid schemes which could help him obtain representation for a court appeal or MHRT. Transferred patients should be told about any special MHRT rights.

276   The information required under Sections 132(1) and 132(2) must be given both orally and in writing, and the information given in writing must, if practicable, be given to the nearest relative within a reasonable time. Leaflets, containing the minimum information to be given to the patient, are available from DHSS Health Publication Unit, in order to assist the hospital managers fulfil their responsibilities under the Act (see Appendix 4). An oral explanation is required because this will often be the best way of helping the patient to understand his position. The nurse, doctor or other professional who explains the patient's rights to him should answer all reasonable questions, and should explain these matters to the patient in an appropriate way bearing in mind the patient's intelligence and any hearing disabilities or linguistic problems. For example, it should not be presumed that oral/aural and written methods will meet the needs of hearing impaired patients. In

such cases the assistance of a local authority or voluntary agency social worker with the deaf may be necessary. In the case of the longer term powers a period of time may be allowed to elapse before the patient is given this information if, at the start of detention, his condition is so bad that it is felt he will not understand it, but it is important that this delay is not prolonged until it conflicts with the requirements of the law to inform 'as soon as practicable'. If leaflets in translation are required enquiries should be made of DHSS Priority Care Division.

277   When a patient is discharged from detention, or the authority for his detention expires, this fact should be made clear to him, whether he wishes to leave or to stay on as an informal patient. Arrangements should be made for a member of staff or a social worker to see a patient who is to be discharged in order to make arrangements for his aftercare and tell him of his rights under the Homeless Persons Act 1977 and other relevant legislation.

Duty of managers to inform nearest relative of discharge

278   Section 133 requires that where a patient is to be discharged from hospital or a mental nursing home, other than by an order of the nearest relative, the person (if any) appearing to be the nearest relative should be informed, within 7 days if practicable, of the patient's discharge, unless the patient or the relative has asked that such information should not be given.

Patient's correspondence

279   Section 134 provides power for detained patients' incoming or out-going mail to be inspected and withheld. There are no restrictions on voluntary patients' correspondence. A 'postal packet' has the same meaning in Section 134 as it does in the Post Office Act 1953 which is: 'a letter, postcard, reply postcard, newspaper, printed packet or parcel and every packet or article transmissible by post (which includes a telegram).'

280   A postal packet addressed by any detained patient may be withheld from the Post Office if the person to whom it is addressed has asked that he should receive no correspondence from that patient (Section 134(1)(a)). A request from a person that correspondence addressed to him by the patient should be withheld must be in writing, and must be given to the hospital managers, the rmo or the Secretary of State. Any power to withhold a postal packet in that Section applies also to any item contained in a postal packet. If

appropriate, an item from a packet can be withheld and the rest of the packet forwarded to the addressee (see Section 134(4)).

281   Section 134(1)(*b*) applies only to special hospitals and provides that a postal packet can be withheld from the Post Office if it is likely to cause distress to the person to whom it is addressed or to any other person who is not on the staff of the hospital, or to cause danger to any person. It is intended that this power should be used to withhold for example, threatening letters, letters to victims of crime, or dangerous objects. Section 132(2) also applies only to special hospitals. It allows the managers of special hospitals (or a member of staff appointed by them) to withhold a postal packet from a patient if they believe it is necessary to do so in the interests of the safety of the patient or for the protection of other persons.

282   Section 134(3) modifies the powers mentioned in para 281 above so that postal packets cannot be withheld if they are addressed to a patient by or on behalf of certain people or bodies, or if sent by the patient to those people or bodies.

The people or bodies concerned are:
a.   any Government Minister or Member of Parliament;
b.   the Master or any other officer of the Court of Protection or any of the Lord Chancellor's Visitors;
c.   the Parliamentary Commissioner, the Health Service Commissioner for England or for Wales or a Local Commissioner;
d.   a Mental Health Review Tribunal;
e.   a health authority (including the Mental Health Act Commission), local social services authority, Community Health Council or probation or after care committee;
f.   the managers of the hospital where the patient is detained;
g.   the patient's legal adviser (if legally qualified and instructed by the patient to act for him);
h.   the European Commission of Human Rights or the European Court of Human Rights.

283   The managers of a hospital, or a person appointed by them, may inspect or open any postal packet to see whether it is one to which Sections 134(1) and (2) apply and if so, whether it or anything contained in it, should be withheld. In hospitals other than special hospitals it will not be necessary to open correspondence, only to look at the address. In special hospitals it may be necessary to open both outgoing and incoming letters to determine whether Section 134(1) or (2) apply. (Postal packets should only be opened when there is a suspicion that these Sections do apply.)

Procedure for inspecting correspondence

284 Regulation 17 describes the procedure which should be followed if a postal packet is inspected and opened. Inspection alone does not have to be recorded: this includes cases where the contents can be read without opening (ie in the case of a postcard). If a packet is opened but nothing is withheld, the person who opened the packet must place a notice in the packet stating:

a. that the packet has been opened and inspected;
b. that nothing has been withheld;
c. his name and the name of the hospital.

285 Where a postal packet or item contained in it is withheld, a record must be made in a register kept for the purpose by the person who withheld it of:

i.   the fact that the package or item in it has been withheld;
ii.   the date and the grounds on which it was withheld;
iii. the name of the appointed person who withheld it;
iv.   a description of the item withheld.

If anything in a packet is withheld, but the package is allowed to go on to the addressee, a notice should be placed in the packet stating:

i.   that the packet has been opened and inspected and an item withheld;
ii.   the grounds on which the item has been withheld;
iii. the name of the appointed person who withheld it;
iv.   a description of the item withheld;
v.   the effect of subsections 7 and 8 of Section 121.

((ii) and (v) do not apply in Section 134(i)(*a*) cases)

Where a whole postal packet is withheld, the addressee must be sent a notice stating (ii), (iii), (iv) and (v) above and the fact that the packet has been withheld. Any item withheld must be kept safe for a period of six months after which it should, if practicable, be returned to the sender. The police should be informed if a dangerous item is withheld.

Mental Health Act Commission's power to review a decision to withhold post

286 Section 121(7) gives the Mental Health Act Commission power to review any decision to withhold a postal packet under Sections 134(1)(*b*) or (2) provided an application to review such a decision is made within six months of the receipt of the written notice. Such an application should be made to an office of the Commission, and the applicant should provide the Commission with a copy of the written notice. In the case of outgoing mail it

is only the special hospital patient who may apply, but in the case of incoming mail, the special hospital patient or the sender may apply. When reviewing a decision to withhold a postal packet the Commission may inspect documents and evidence (including the withheld item) which it reasonably requires. The Commission has the power to release the withheld item to the addressee (Section 121(8)).

Managers' power to appoint staff to inspect post

287 The managers of a hospital can appoint such staff or categories of staff as they think fit to inspect and withhold post. It is expected that the decision to withhold post would be made in consultation with the rmo.

Assistance from the police to retake patients or to remove them to a place of safety

288 Police constables are included among the people authorised to retake patients who are absent without leave from the hospital where they are liable to be detained or from the place where they are required by their guardian to live (Section 18). They are also included among the people authorised by Section 138 to retake patients who escape while being conveyed from one place to another, or who escape from a place of safety or custody under the Act.

289 Calls on the police to assist in the retaking of patients should be kept to a minimum, but the police should always be informed at once of the escape or absence without leave of a patient who is considered dangerous or who is subject to restriction on discharge under Part III of the Act. There may be other cases where, although it is not necessary to seek help from the police in retaking a patient, his history makes it desirable that the police should be informed that he is absent without leave in the area. Whenever the police are asked for help in retaking a patient they must be informed of the time limit on the power to retake him.

290 Section 135 provides powers of entry on a magistrate's warrant to obtain access to a patient in the circumstances described in Section 135(1)(a) and (b). Such a warrant will name a constable. Section 135(4) requires that when a constable executes a warrant he must be accompanied by a doctor and approved social worker. The doctor will be able to advise whether the patient should be removed to a place of safety pending an application under Part II of the Act. A place of safety is defined as residential accommodation provided by a local social services authority (under Part III of the National

Assistance Act 1948 or under paragraph 2 of Schedule 8 to the National Health Service Act 1971), a hospital, police station, mental nursing home, residential home for the mentally disordered or any other suitable place where the occupier is willing temporarily to receive the patient.

291   If the patient is removed to a place of safety he may be kept there for not more than 72 hours while other arrangements are made. Only in exceptional circumstances should a police station be used as a place of safety. If a police station is used, the patient should remain there for no longer than a few hours while an approved social worker makes the necessary arrangements for his removal elsewhere, either informally or under Part II of the Act.

292   Section 135(2) provides for the issue of a warrant to take or retake a patient who has escaped or who is absent without leave. When a constable executes the warrant he may be accompanied by a doctor or any other person who is already authorised to retake the patient. The person who is authorised to retake the patient should normally accompany the constable and then take the patient direct to the hospital or place where he is required to live.

293   Police constables also have the power under Section 136 to remove to a place of safety a person whom they find in a public place who appears to be suffering from mental disorder and to be in immediate need of care and control in his own interests or for the protection of others. The patient should be taken to the nearest convenient place of safety (as defined in Section 135(6)) where he can be medically examined and suitable arrangements made for his care. The police, if they do not take the patient direct to hospital, will contact an approved social worker who should make suitable arrangements for the placement of the patient as soon as possible.

Detention of MPs and Members of the House of Lords

294   Section 141(1) provides that when a member of the House of Commons is detained under the Act the following bodies or persons all have a duty to inform the Speaker of the House of Commons at the Palace of Westminster, London SW1 that the detention of that MP has been authorised:
a.   the court, authority or person who made the order or application for detention;
b.   the registered medical practitioners making medical recommendations;

c. the managers of the hospital or mental nursing home or other place where the MP is detained.

295   There is no similar provision in the Act for members of the House of Lords but House of Lords Standing Order 77 requires a court or authority ordering the imprisonment or restraint of a member of the House of Lords to give written notice to the Clerk of the Parliaments. Where a member of the House of Lords is detained under the Act, the managers of the hospital or mental nursing home where that member is detained should inform the Clerk of the Parliaments, House of Lords, SW1 in writing of the Section of the Act under which that member is detained and the date of his detention. The Clerk should also be informed when the member of the House of Lords is discharged or given leave of absence, or if he absents himself without leave. Where the member of the House of Lords is sent from a court or transferred from prison, the court or prison will have informed the Clerk of the Parliaments but when that member is discharged or given leave of absence, or if he absents himself from the hospital or nursing home without leave, it will be for the managers to inform the Clerk.

Protection for acts done in pursuance of the Act

296   Section 139 gives protection against litigation to persons acting in pursuance of the Act or any regulations or rules made under the Act so long as the act in question was not done in bad faith or without reasonable care. The Section also covers acts purporting to be done in pursuance of the Act, and acts done under other legislation relating to the Court of Protection. Criminal proceedings against staff require the consent of the Director of Public Prosecutions and civil proceedings require the consent of the High Court. It is not necessary, as it was under the 1959 Act, to show that there is 'substantial grounds' for the contention that staff acted in bad faith or without reasonable care. Nevertheless, the Director of Public Prosecutions and the High Court, in granting consent or leave, will apply their own rules which require grounds to be demonstrated. Section 139 does not apply to the Secretary of State or to health authorities.

Sexual Offences against Patients

297   Section 128 of the Mental Health Act 1959 is not repealed by the 1983 Act and continues to have effect, as amended by the Sexual Offences Act 1967. The Section makes it an offence for a man to have 'unlawful sexual intercourse' with a woman or commit homosexual acts with another man, if

he is employed in a hospital or mental nursing home where the woman or man is being treated for mental disorder, or if he is the guardian of the mentally disordered person, or if the person is otherwise in his custody or care under the Act, and under certain other circumstances (Section 128(1)). The Section should be construed as one with the Sexual Offences Act 1956 (Section 128(5)). Where there is reason to believe that an offence has been committed under this Section, the Chief Constable should be informed as soon as possible. The police will then decide what is the right course, in consultation with the doctor in charge of the patient's treatment where the patient is resident in or on leave of absence from the hospital (except when the doctor is named as the assailant).

298   It is no longer necessary to advise DHSS or Welsh Office of action taken under Section 128 of the Mental Health Act 1959.

Schedule 5   Transitional and saving provisions

Transitional provisions – Introduction

299   Schedule 5 makes provision to cover the transition from the 1959 Act, as amended by the 1982 Act, to the 1983 Act, and therefore affects patients detained on and before 30 September 1983 and anything which was in the process of being done at that date. The interpretation of consolidating legislation is largely governed by the Interpretation Act 1978 but Schedule 5 makes some additional specific provisions (for example, paragraphs 1–3, 21–28, 32 and 46 of Schedule 5). In addition, Schedule 5 repeats transitional and saving provisions which were made in the 1982 Act, suitably adapted (see for example paragraphs 4–20 of Schedule 5) and those which were made in the 1959 Act, again suitably adapted, which are still relevant (see for example, paragraphs 29–31, 33–45 of Schedule 5).

General transitional provisions

300   Where a period of time specified in the old legislation has begun to run before 30 September 1983, so that it straddles that day, the duration of that period is to be calculated under the corresponding provisions of the new legislation. Thus if the period specified in the new legislation is of the same duration as that specified in the old legislation the duration remains the same. Otherwise the new period applies (paragraph 1, Schedule 5). The exceptions to this are described below, and include the duration of the authority to detain for treatment for which there are special arrangements.

301   Those provisions of the 1959 Act which have not been consolidated into the Act (namely Sections 8, 9, 128 and other supplemental provisions) are to be interpreted by the use of the names and definitions of mental disorders in Section 1 of the 1983 Act and the definitions in Section 145(1) of the 1983 Act (paragraph 2, Schedule 5).

302   Continuity between the old legislation and the new legislation is ensured by paragraph 3, Schedule 5. In particular, this paragraph ensures

that something done under, or the purpose of, the old legislation does not simply cease to have effect because of the repeal of the old legislation. For example, detention for treatment authorised under the 1959 Act which is current at 30 September 1983 is automatically treated as if it had been authorised under the new legislation (there is however specific provision for the authority for detention or for guardianship which is described below).

Specific transitional provisions for detention or guardianship

303   Paragraphs 6 and 7 of Schedule 5 ensure the continuing validity of applications made under the 1959 Act. Paragraph 6 ensures that the changes in the definitions of mental disorder will not affect the authority to detain somebody who was detained prior to 30 September 1983. This paragraph does not apply to the renewal of authority.

304   Paragraph 7 ensures that any application made before 30 September 1983 will be valid for the full 14 days, and it will therefore still constitute the authority to convey or detain the patient as appropriate, or will confer guardianship. The old time limits will apply to emergency applications made before 30 September 1983. However, if an application has not been signed before 30 September 1983 it must fulfil all the requirements of the new Act. It must therefore be in the new form, and must be supported by recommendations in the new form reflecting the new criteria. If an applicant has obtained a medical recommendation in the form required by the 1959 Act before 30 September 1983 he must make his application before that date. However, there is nothing to prevent a medical recommendation being made in the new form before 30 September 1983 so long as the application is made no earlier than that day.

305   When an authority to detain a patient admitted for treatment or to subject a patient to guardianship is renewed before 1 October 1983 the duration of the authority applicable under the 1959 Act (of one or two years) will continue to apply. However, where the authority has been renewed for two years and less than 16 months has passed since the renewal by 30 September 1983, that period of detention will expire after 18 months rather than 2 years. If that detention is subsequently renewed the period of one year will apply (Section 20, Schedule 5, paragraph 9).

306   **If a person under 16 is subject to guardianship on 30 September 1983 the authority for guardianship will cease on that day** (Schedule 5, paragraph 8(1)). Local social services authorities should consider in advance of 30 September 1983 what other arrangements they will want to make for this person. In other cases, where guardianship continues after 30 September,

paragraph 8(2) of Schedule 5 ensures that Section 8(1) which limits the power of guardian to the 'three essential powers' applies (see para 46).

Role of nearest relative

307 Paragraph 11 of Schedule 5 provides a saving to ensure that an application to a Mental Health Review Tribunal does not lapse when Section 26 of the Act comes into force. The effect of this paragraph is that an applicant to a Tribunal who was the patient's nearest relative under the terms of the 1959 Act can continue with an application although he may not be the nearest relative under the terms of the 1983 Act. Any subsequent application would have to be made by the nearest relative as defined in Section 26 (para 67). Where a patient is being detained under Section 25 of the 1959 Act on 30 September, the nearest relative will not have the power of discharge under Section 23(2)(*a*) (paragraph 10, Schedule 5).

Effect of new consent to treatment provisions on patients detained before 30 September 1983

308 The provisions in Section 58 for consent to certain treatments are not to apply until 1 April 1984 to any treatment given to a patient whose detention began before 30 September 1983. The procedure described in Section 58 (para 196 et seq) must immediately be followed on 1 April in a case where a patient has received medicine on or before 1 January during that period of detention. The Section 57 provisions apply to any patient from 30 September 1983.

Application of Sections 126 and 139 before 30 September 1983

309 Section 126 of the 1983 Act applies to applications, recommendations, reports and other documents to which the 1959 Act applied before 30 September 1983. Similarly, Section 139 of the 1983 Act applies to acts to which Section 141 of 1959 Act applied when it was in force (paragraph 28, Schedule 5).

Duty of managers to give information

310 A patient detained at the time the Act comes into force must be given the information required under Section 132 (para 274 et seq) as soon as practicable and so must his nearest relative or the person acting as such. He

should, in effect, be treated as a new patient for the purposes of Section 132, but he and his nearest relative must be informed of any transitional provisions which modify any of the provisions referred to in Section 132 in his particular case (paragraph 19, Schedule 5).

Provisions relating to the detention of people detained under Schedule 6 of the Mental Health Act 1959

311 The authority to detain a patient, or subject him to guardianship, by virtue of paragraph 9 of Schedule 6 of the 1959 Act is not affected by the commencement of the 1983 Act (paragraph 31 of Schedule 5) for the remainder of the patients' 'current period of treatment'.[1] The patients this paragraph refers to are patients who prior to 1 November 1960 were:
a. subject to reception orders under the Lunacy Act 1890 (other than urgency orders) or to orders under other Acts which had the same effect as reception orders;
b. temporary patients under the Mental Treatment Act 1930;
c. patients detained or subject to guardianship under the Mental Deficiency Act 1913 other than those detained under Section 15 or detained on remand under Section 8(4), or those detained under Section 9 whose period of detention in a penal establishment or approved school had not yet expired.

These patients may apply to a Mental Health Review Tribunal before the expiry of their period of treatment (paragraph 31(2) of Schedule 5)).

312 Similarly, paragraph 32 of Schedule 5 provides that patients described in 311(a)–(c) above whose authority for detention or guardianship has been renewed under paragraph 11 of Schedule 6 of the 1959 Act, can continue to be detained for the period of that authority after 30 September 1983.

313 Paragraph 33 of Schedule 5 makes further provisions for the patients described in paragraphs 31 and 32. The authority for their detention can be renewed for a further two years when it expires, which in the case of any patients described in paragraph 32 will be after two years. The conditions for renewal are the same as those for patients detained for treatment or subject to guardianship under the current legislation (as set out in Sections 20(3) to 20(10)). Forms 30 or 31 must be used to renew the authority for detention or guardianship (Regulation 10). However, as such patients can be detained for two years, the effect of Section 66(1)(f) is that they can only make one

---

[1] Defined in paragraph 42(1)(a) of Schedule 5. This refers to the period for which the patient would have remained liable to detention (or subject to guardianship) on 1 November 1960 if the legislation he was detained under had been unaltered by the 1959 Act.

application to a Mental Health Review Tribunal in the two year period (unless an opportunity arises from another provision).

314 A patient detained, or subject to guardianship by virtue of paragraph 31 of Schedule 5 should be treated as if he were admitted for treatment or placed under guardianship under the 1983 Act, with the exceptions mentioned above. A further exception to this is that where any patient was detained before 1 November 1960 under Section 6, 8(1) or 9 of the Mental Deficiency Act 1913 the nearest relative does not have the power of discharge under Section 23. However, he may apply to a Mental Health Review Tribunal once during each 12 month period of detention (paragraph 34(4) of Schedule 5).

315 Anyone who was a guardian before 1 November 1960 and continued as one under paragraph 14 of Schedule 6 of the 1959 Act can continue by virtue of paragraph 36 after 30 September 1983.

316 A patient who was detained prior to 1 November 1960 under Section 20, 21 or 21(a) of the Lunacy Act 1980 may continue to be detained until the end of his period of treatment current on 1 November 1960 unless he is detained or made subject to guardianship under the 1983 Act prior to that (Paragraph 40 of Schedule 5).

Transitional provisions relating to Tribunals

317 Paragraph 12 ensures that any patient aged under 16 who was admitted to hospital for treatment, received into guardianship or made subject to a hospital order before 30 September 1983 does not lose any right to apply to a Tribunal which he might have had under the 1959 Act (ie under Sections 31(4), 34(5) or 63(4)(a) of the 1959 Act).

318 Paragraph 13 states that Section 68(1) of the Act does not apply to any patient admitted or transferred before 31 March 1983. If a patient detained after that date does not exercise his right to apply to a Tribunal the automatic referral procedure described in paragraphs 209–210 comes into force. In the case of the renewal of detention or of patients aged under 16 the automatic referral procedure comes into force on 30 September 1983.

319 Paragraph 14 ensures that patients detained by virtue of a hospital order between 31 March and 30 September 1983 retain their right to a Tribunal in the first six months of detention.

Transfer directions with restrictions

320 The new provisions relating to the cases where a transfer direction together with a restriction direction is given in respect of a prisoner found to

be suffering from mental disorder (sections 50–53) apply to such a direction given before 30 September 1983 as well as to those given after that date. A restriction direction in respect of a person serving a fixed term of imprisonment which under Section 50(3) would have expired before 30 September 1983 will instead expire on that date (paragraph 15 of Schedule 5); Section 77(4) of the 1959 Act will continue to apply (with the necessary modifications) to a transfer direction given before 30 September 1983 (paragraph 20 of Schedule 5); and the effect of any transfer under section 71 of the 1959 Act will be preserved by Section 46(3) of the 1983 Act (paragraph 21 of Schedule 5).

Restricted patients

321   The new criteria in Section 42(1) for the termination by the Home Secretary of a restriction order, and the new rights of direct access to the Mental Health Review Tribunal for restricted patients, will apply to all such patients irrespective of when the restrictions were imposed, except that for the purpose of calculating a patient's entitlement to apply to the Tribunal any previous reference of his case to the Tribunal will be treated as an application by the patient, and the provision for automatic reference of certain cases by the Home Secretary within specified time limits will not be relevant where those time limits have already expired by 30 September 1983 (paragraph 16 of Schedule 5). A hospital order patient subject to restrictions who has been removed from the United Kingdom under Section 90 of the 1959 Act will not remain liable to detention on his return as would be the case under the terms of Section 91(2) of the 1983 Act (paragraph 17 of Schedule 5).

322   The authority for the continued detention of patients whose detention commenced under pre-1959 Act legislation and was preserved by paragraph 15 of Schedule 6 to that Act is provided by paragraph 37 of Schedule 5 to the 1983 Act, which also specifies the Sections of the Act corresponding to the provisions of the 1959 Act which governed such patient's detention. Paragraph 38 makes similar provision in respect of such patients who have been conditionally discharged, and paragraph 39 makes provision (corresponding to paragraph 17 of Schedule 6 to the 1959 Act) for the procedure on expiration of restrictions in such cases.

Appendix 1
Addresses of Mental Health Act Commission Offices

Mental Health Act Commission
Cressington House
249 St Mary's Road
Garston
Liverpool L19 0NF

Tel: 051–427 2061

This office covers:
North Western, Mersey and West
Midlands RHAs.
Clwyd, Gwynedd and Powys
Health Authorities.
Park Lane and Moss Side Special
Hospitals.

Mental Health Act Commission
3rd Floor
Maid Marian House
Houndsgate
Nottingham NG1 6BG

Tel: 0602 410304

This office covers:
Northern, Yorkshire and Trent
RHAs.
Rampton Special Hospital.

Mental Health Act Commission
Floor 1
Hepburn House
Marsham Street
London SW1P 4HW

Tel: 01–211 8061/211 8954

This office covers:
East Anglian, NW Thames,
NE Thames, SE Thames,
SW Thames, Oxford, Wessex and
South Western RHAs.
Pembrokeshire, East Dyfed,
W Glamorgan, Mid Glamorgan,
S Glamorgan and Gwent Health
Authorities.
Broadmoor Special Hospital.

(The London office also provides
support for the Chairman and the
Central Policy Committee)

Appendix 2

Addresses of the Mental Health Review Tribunals

Clerk to the Nottingham Tribunal
Office
Spur A Block 5
Government Buildings
Chalfont Drive
Western Boulevard
Nottingham NG8 3RZ

Tel: 0602 294222/3

This office covers:
Northern, Yorkshire and Trent
RHAs.
Rampton Special Hospital.

Clerk to the Mersey Tribunal
Office
Floor 3
Cressington House
249 St Mary's Road
Garston
Liverpool L19 0NF

Tel: 051–494 0095

This office covers:
North Western, Mersey and West
Midlands RHAs.
Park Lane and Moss Side Special
Hospitals.

Clerk to the London Tribunal
Office
Floor 15
Euston Tower
Euston Road
London NW1 3DN

Tel: 01–388 1188 Ext 3787/6

This office covers:
East Anglian, NW Thames,
NE Thames, SE Thames,
SW Thames, Oxford, Wessex and
South Western RHAs.
Broadmoor Special Hospital.

Clerk to the Welsh Tribunal Office
2nd Floor
New Crown Building
Cathays Park
Cardiff CF1 3NQ

Tel: 0222 825798

This office covers:
Wales

Appendix 3
Law Society – Legal Aid Centres in England and Wales

No 1   London South
The Law Society
No 1 Legal Aid Area
29/37 Red Lion Street
London WC1R 4PP
Tel: 01–405 6991

No 2   South Eastern
The Law Society
No 2 Legal Aid Area
9–12 Middle Street
Brighton BN1 1AS
Tel: 0273 27003

No 3   Southern
The Law Society
No 3 Legal Aid Area
80 King's Road
Reading RG1 4LT
Tel: 0734 589696

No 4   South Western
The Law Society
No 4 Legal Aid Area
Whitefriars (Block C)
Lewins Mead
Bristol BS1 2LR
Tel: 0272 214801

No 5   South Wales
The Law Society
No 5 Legal Aid Area
Marland House
Central Square
Cardiff CF1 1PF
Tel: 0222 388971

No 6   West Midland
The Law Society
No 6 Legal Aid Area
Podium Centre City
5 Hill Street
Birmingham B5 4UD
Tel: 021–632 6541

No 7   North Western
The Law Society
No 7 Legal Aid Area
Elisabeth House
16 St Peter's Square
Manchester M2 3DA
Tel: 061–228 1200

No 8   Northern
The Law Society
No 8 Legal Aid Area
Eagle Star House
Fenkle Street
Newcastle Upon Tyne
NE1 5RU
Tel: 0632 323461

No 9   North Eastern
The Law Society
No 9 Legal Aid Area
City House
New Station Street
Leeds LS1 4JS
Tel: 0532 442851

No 10   East Midland
The Law Society
No 10 Legal Aid Area
5 Friar Lane
Nottingham
NG1 6BW
Tel: 0602 412424

No 11   Eastern
The Law Society
No 11 Legal Aid Area
Kett House
Station Road
Cambridge CB1 2JT
Tel: 0223 66511

**No 12   Chester and
North Wales**
The Law Society
No 12 Legal Aid Area
2nd Floor
Pepper House
Pepper Road
Chester CH1 1DW
Tel: 0244 315455

No 13   London East
The Law Society
No 13 Legal Aid Area
29/37 Red Lion Street
London WC1R 4PP
Tel: 01–405 6991

No 14   London West
The Law Society
No 14 Legal Aid Area
29/37 Red Lion Street
London WC1R 4PP
Tel: 01–405 6991

No 15   Merseyside
The Law Society
No 15 Legal Aid Area
Moor House
James Street
Liverpool L2 7SA
Tel: 051–236 8371

Legal Aid Areas

Area No 1
London South
The London Boroughs
   of
Bexley
Bromley
Croydon
Ealing
Greenwich
Hounslow
Kingston
Lambeth
Lewisham
Merton
Richmond
Southwark
Sutton
Wandsworth

Area No 2
South Eastern
East Sussex
Kent
Surrey
West Sussex

Area No 3
Southern
Berkshire
Buckinghamshire
Dorset
Hampshire
Isle of Wight
Oxfordshire

Area No 4
South Western
Avon
Cornwall
Devon
Gloucestershire
Somerset
Wiltshire

Area No 5
South Wales
Dyfed
Gwent
Mid Glamorgan
South Glamorgan
West Glamorgan

The following districts
   in Powys:
Brecknock
Radnor

Area No 6
West Midland
Hereford & Worcester
Warwickshire
West Midlands

The following districts
  in Staffordshire:
Cannock Chase
Lichfield
South Staffordshire
Tamworth

Area No 7
North Western
The following districts
  in Cumbria:
Barrow-in-Furness
South Lakeland

The following districts
  in Greater
  Manchester:
Bolton
Bury
Manchester
Oldham
Rochdale
Salford
Stockport
Tameside
Trafford
Wigan

The following districts
  in Lancashire:
Blackburn
Burnley
Chorley
Hyndburn
Lancaster
Pendle
Ribble Valley
Rossendale

Area No 8
Northern
Cleveland
Durham
Northumberland
Tyne & Wear

The following districts
  in Cumbria:
Allerdale
Carlisle
Copeland
Eden

The following districts
  in North Yorkshire:
Hambleton
Richmondshire
Ryedale
Scarborough

Area No 9
North Eastern
South Yorkshire
West Yorkshire

The following districts
  in Humberside:
Beverley
Boothferry
Holderness
Kingston-upon-Hull
North Wolds

The following districts
  in North Yorkshire:
Craven
Harrogate
Selby
York

Area No 10
East Midland
Derbyshire
Leicestershire
Lincolnshire
Northamptonshire
Nottinghamshire

The following districts
  in Humberside:
Cleethorpes
Glanford
Grimsby
Scunthorpe

Area No 11
Eastern
Bedfordshire
Cambridgeshire
Essex
Hertfordshire
Norfolk
Suffolk

Area No 12
*Chester and North
  Wales*
Clwyd
Gwynedd
Shropshire

The following districts
  in Cheshire:
Chester
Congleton
Crewe and Nantwich
Ellesmere Port
Halton
Macclesfield
Vale Royal
Warrington

The following districts
in Powys:
Montgomery

The following districts
in Staffordshire:
East Staffordshire
Newcastle-under-
  Lyme
Stafford
Staffordshire Moors
Stoke-on-Trent

Area No 13
London East
The City of London
The London Boroughs
  of
Barking
Camden
Hackney
Havering
Islington
Newham
Redbridge
Tower Hamlets
Waltham Forest

Area No 14
London West
the London Boroughs
  of
Barnet
Brent
Enfield
Hammersmith
Haringey
Harrow
Hillingdon
Kensington and
  Chelsea
Westminster

Area No 15
Merseyside
Merseyside

The following districts
  in Lancashire:
Blackpool
Fylde
Preston
South Ribble
Wyre
West Lancashire

Appendix 4
Mental Health Act 1983   Patients' leaflets

The Mental Health Act 1983 Section number appears in bold type after each entry

ADMISSION TO HOSPITAL	Leaflet Number
Admission for assessment in cases of emergency **S4**	2
Admission for assessment **S2**	6
Admission for treatment **S3**	7
Admission of patients removed by police following court warrant **S135**	4
Admission of mentally disordered persons found in public places **S136**	5

ADMISSION TO HOSPITAL VIA THE COURTS	
Hospital orders – details of implications of being admitted to hospital through a court order **S37**	8
Restriction orders – details of implications of being admitted to hospital through court order with restriction under Section 41 **S37+41**	9
Patients admitted to hospital through court order – Rights to Appeal **S37 and S37+41**	12

GUARDIANSHIP

PATIENTS ALREADY IN HOSPITAL

The Mental Health Act 1983 leaflets are non statutory (see paragraph 276) and are produced by the Department of Health and Social Security. They are available from:

Department of Health and Social Security
Health Publications Unit
No 2 Site
Manchester Road
Heywood
Lancs OL10 2PZ

Mental Health Act 1983   Statutory forms

The Mental Health Act 1983 Section number appears in bold type after each entry

APPLICATIONS BY APPROVED SOCIAL WORKERS	Form Number
For admission for assessment **S2**	2
For emergency admission for assessment **S4**	6
For admission for treatment **S3**	9
For guardianship **S7**	18

APPLICATIONS BY NEAREST RELATIVE	
For admission for assessment **S2**	1
For emergency admission for assessment **S4**	5
For admission for treatment **S3**	8
For guardianship **S7**	17

MEDICAL RECOMMENDATIONS	
For admission for assessment **S2**	4
For emergency admission for assessment **S4**	7
For admission for treatment **S3**	11
For reception into guardianship **S7**	20
For transfer from guardianship **S19**	29

JOINT MEDICAL RECOMMENDATIONS

HOSPITAL REPORTS

HOSPITAL RECORDS

CLASSIFICATION OF PATIENT

RECLASSIFICATION OF PATIENT

DISCHARGE BY NEAREST RELATIVE

RENEWAL OF AUTHORITY

CONSENT TO TREATMENT

AUTHORITY FOR TRANSFER OF A PATIENT

The Mental Health Act 1983 Statutory Forms are found in Schedule 1 in SI 1983 No 893: 'The Mental Health (Hospital, Guardianship and Consent to Treatment) Regulations 1983'.

These forms are produced by the Department of Health and Social Security.

Forms for Health Authorities are available from:

Department of Health and Social Security
DPSU
Room 110
North Fylde Central Offices
Norcross
Blackpool
Lancs FY5 3TA

Forms for Social Services Authorities are available from:

Department of Health and Social Security
Health Publications Unit
No 2 Site
Manchester Road
Heywood
Lancs OL10 2PZ

Appendix 5
Mental Health Act 1983: Part VI

Procedural guide on the removal of detained patients to and from Scotland and Northern Ireland (Paragraphs 236–247)

This is a brief summary only, acting as an aide memoire; the advice cannot be authoritative in matters of law.

1   Informal Patients   There are no formal requirements where an informal patient is to be transferred to or from Scotland or Northern Ireland, but confirmation should be obtained that a receiving hospital is content with the arrangements and that the patient is willing to go.

2   Transfer to Scotland or Northern Ireland of a Detained Patient   The Act provides that such a transfer can take place only where:
a.   a transfer is in the interests of the patient;
b.   arrangements have been made for admission and
c.   the Secretary of State has so authorised the transfer.

3   Transfer to Scotland or Northern Ireland of patients other than restricted patients (Mental Health Act 1983, Sections 2, 3 and 37 or 47 without an order or warrant restricting discharge)

Once transfer has been agreed in principle the sending hospital should write to:

Priority Care Division
Branch PC4D
Room C519
Department of Health and Social Security
Alexander Fleming House
Elephant and Castle
London
SE1 6BY
(01–407 5522 Ext 6228)

The sending hospital should include in this:
a. patient's full name
b section of the Act under which he is detained
c. name of the receiving hospital
d. name of doctor agreeing to receive the patient
e. reasons why transfer is considered to be in the patient's best interests.
Sufficient time should be allowed for arrangements to be checked with the receiving country and for the written authority of the Secretary of State to be issued. It will speed matters if a copy of a letter from the proposed receiving hospital confirming willingness to accept the patient can be supplied.

4 Transfer to Scotland or Northern Ireland of a restricted patient (Mental Health Act 1983, Sections 37 with 41 and 47 with 49; also, patients detained under the Criminal Procedure (Insanity) Act 1964)

Full details of the proposed transfer should be sent to:

C3 Division
Home Office
Queen Anne's Gate
London
SW1H 9AT
(01–213 3206)

5   General Matters

The escort accompanying the patient must take with the patient the documents authorising detention of the patient under the Mental Health Act 1983 and the formal authority for transfer. Where they are to travel by public transport it will often be appropriate as a matter of courtesy to inform the carrier of the arrangements in advance in order that necessary reassurance as to the patient's likely conduct can be given. This is particularly so where the travel is to be by air.

6   Transfer from Scotland or Northern Ireland of a Detained Patient

Before finalising arrangements for reception, confirm that the sending hospital has sought formal authority for the transfer from the Scottish Home and Health Department or the Department of Health and Social Services, Northern Ireland, as appropriate. The authority of the appropriate Minister should accompany the other detention documents to be delivered to the hospital managers on the patient's arrival. The Home Office will wish to be involved at an early stage in the case of any patient who will be subject to restrictions on discharge after transfer.

When the patient is admitted, Mental Health Form 33 must be completed on behalf of the managers. The responsible medical officer must record on Form 32 the Mental Health Act 1983 classification of disorder (mental illness, severe mental impairment, mental impairment or psychopathic disorder) as he assesses. Psychopathic disorder is excluded from the definition of mental disorder under the Mental Health (Northern Ireland) Order 1986 (article 3(2)) and under the Mental Health (Scotland) Act 1984 (Section 17(1)(a)(i)).

The patient and nearest relative must be told of any rights of application, or to request a reference, to the Mental Health Review Tribunal, and the managers of the hospital must also give relevant information as indicated by Section 132 of the Mental Health Act 1983.

7   Transfers to and from Scotland or Northern Ireland – a brief guide to the corresponding provisions of the relevant legislation

i.   Patients transferred to England and Wales

When transferred into a hospital in England or Wales the patient is treated as having been admitted under an application, or order or direction made, on the date of admission to hospital in England or Wales (eg detention under Section 3 lasts for six months from admission). Persons detained under respective sections of the Northern Ireland Order or Scotland Act appertaining to detention by virtue of a transfer direction while serving a sentence of imprisonment shall be treated as if the sentence had been imposed by a court in England and Wales. Where such a person prior to transfer to England and Wales was subject to an order or direction restricting his discharge, being an order or direction of limited duration, that order or direction shall expire on the date on which it would have expired if he had not been so transferred to England and Wales.

The patient will be liable to be detained under the provisions of the Mental Health Act 1983 corresponding to that under which he was detained under the Scotland Act or Northern Ireland Order. (See Section 77 of the Mental Health (Scotland) Act 1984 and Section 82 of the Mental Health Act 1983.) The commonest corresponding provisions are set out in Appendix 5, paragraph 8.

ii. Patients transferred to Scotland or Northern Ireland

On arrival the patient will be liable to be detained under the provisions of the Scotland or Northern Ireland legislation corresponding to the particular section of the Mental Health Act 1983 under which the patient was being detained in England or Wales.

8   Corresponding Provisions of the Relevant Legislation

Mental Health (Scotland) Act 1984	Mental Health (Northern Ireland) Order 1986	Mental Health Act 1983 (England and Wales)
Section 18*	Article 4	Section 2
Section 24†		Section 4
Section 18	Article 12	Section 3
Sections 175 or 376 of the Criminal Procedure (Scotland) Act 1975, without restrictions on discharge	Article 44 without restrictions on discharge	Section 37 without restrictions on discharge
Sections 175 or 376 of the Criminal Procedure (Scotland) Act 1975 with a further order under Section 178 or 379 restricting discharge under Section 62(1) of the Mental Health (Scotland) Act 1984	Article 44 with restrictions under Article 47	Section 37 with restrictions on discharge under Section 41
Section 71 (transfer from prison) without restrictions on discharge	Article 53 (transfer of prisoners) without restrictions on discharge	Section 47
Section 71 with restrictions under Section 72	Article 53 with restrictions under Article 55	Section 47 with restrictions under Section 49

* Section 18 of the Mental Health (Scotland) Act 1984 is not the exact equivalent of Section 2 of the Mental Health Act 1983 but will suffice for the purposes of transfer.

† Section 24 of the Mental Health (Scotland) Act 1984 is only a recommendation and not an application for admission and is therefore not the exact equivalent of Section 4 of the Mental Health Act 1983. There is no emergency admission procedure under the Mental Health (Northern Ireland) Order 1986.

Printed in the United Kingdom for Her Majesty's Stationery Office
Dd 291376 C30 3/89 28940